AWESOME
AT BEING
— *Awesome* —

AWESOME
AT BEING
— *Awesome* —

A Self-Help Book
for People Who Hate
Self-Help Books

DANNY PEHAR

www.bpsbooks.com

Co-editors: Donald G. Bastian and Patricia Pehar

Published in 2016 by
BPS Books
Toronto and New York
www.bpsbooks.com
A division of Bastian Publishing Services Ltd.

ISBN 978-1-77236-028-8 (paperback)
ISBN 978-1-77236-029-5 (ePDF)
ISBN 978-1-77236-030-1 (ePUB)

Cataloguing-in-Publication Data available from Library
and Archives Canada.

Cover and text design: Daniel Crack, Kinetics Design, www.kdbooks.ca

Printed in Canada

Contents

AWESOME
AT BEING
Awesome

Preface

WHEN we were kids we believed in the impossible. We wanted to fly, we dreamed of building spaceships and being superheroes. Everything was magic, everything was awesome. But somewhere along the way things changed. We suffered setbacks, disappointments, stresses, losses and failures. We had weight issues, relationship problems, communication problems, money troubles, career troubles and job loss. Eventually the impossible was no longer possible. We lost our awesome.

But what if we could get it back?

We can, and I believe this book is a great way for you to do so. Telling stories from my life and work experience, I take a very practical and modern approach to the ancient philosophy of balancing mind, body and soul. Without having to resort to most self-help books' hocus-pocus thinking or complex psychology, I show, very simply, how strengthening one aspect of your life will help you strengthen the others. Take back one aspect of your life, and you can take them all back.

Awesome at Being Awesome covers a wide range of topics, from weight management to career management, from saving money to saving relationships, from building the perfect résumé to building the perfect speech, from getting through the toughest job interview to getting through the toughest day. You will learn to balance your life and cut out everything you don't need. You'll learn to do an awesome amount of awesome things and how to do them awesomely – and you'll have fun doing it.

Dedication

I dedicate this book to my parents for teaching me to always look for the good, to my cousin for teaching me the importance of balance, to my nephew for teaching me the importance of awesome, and to my wife – for putting up with all of my crazy ideas, for helping me find my voice and for listening to my stories, but mostly for being a part of my stories and for loving me even when I make it hard. Although, honestly, I make it very easy most of the time.

This book is also dedicated to all those people in my life who goofed off with me, fought off bullies with me, celebrated victories with me, jumped into puddles with me, took beatings with me, laughed with me, cried with me, partied with me, were poor with me, made wishes with me, looked for work with me, succeeded with me, failed with me, got lost with me and imagined with me – and to all those who have inspired me and given me hope when I needed it, whether they knew it or not.

I'm blessed to have been surrounded by so many people who love me and make my life awesome.

As for those of you who find yourself alone with more losses than wins, who feel your life is not awesome at all, this book is especially dedicated to you.

1

My First Life Lesson

I grew up with Eastern European immigrant parents. We didn't have much, but most of the time we were pretty happy. Sometimes, however, it outright sucked.

Like many kids in similar situations, all of my things were hand-me-downs, which I suppose isn't too bad, except for the fact that I had two older sisters. No, I didn't wear any dresses to school, but, yes, on occasion I did have to wear clothing originally meant for them. Every now and then this was very bad news for me – but great news for kids who wanted to make fun of me.

One of the most dreaded T-shirts in my hand-me-down wardrobe, clearly meant for a young girl, had the caption "I love Bon Jovi" with a picture of his face in the middle of a huge pink heart. Wearing it was my way of telling bullies, "If you're not feeling creative today, don't worry about it. I'm gonna make this really easy on you." And I'm sure I don't have to tell you it's pretty hard to muster up the strength to fight back and prove your toughness when you're wearing an "I love Bon Jovi" T-shirt.

Worse than the shirt were my skates. My school had an ice skating program, and my parents insisted I didn't need to buy my own skates for it. They figured, like always, I could make do with something previously used by my sisters. The fact that all girls' skates were white and all boys' skates were black didn't matter to them if it meant saving some money.

At first I didn't think it would be so bad. After all, the white skates certainly went well with most of my other teen girl outfits. Besides, what else could the kids in school possibly say to me that they hadn't already said? What I didn't take into consideration, however, is that growing up in Canada, a place where we love our hockey (everyone but me, for obvious reasons), means you can't be a boy with white skates.

Now, even without the girls' T-shirts, pants and socks, I was horribly uncool. But the skates put things over the top. After repeated begging on my part, my parents felt bad that all the kids were making fun of me. But they thought it would be crazy to part with cash just because of color. They repeatedly said, "Color doesn't matter. All that matters is what's inside." Sounds like a great line for race relations, but they said it only because they were incredibly cheap.

To shut me up without spending any money, my dad painted my skates black, which I thought was brilliant. I went around school bragging to anyone who had ever made fun of me that my parents had come into a bunch of money and bought me new skates. I even threw in a comment about how the only reason I was still wearing the "I Love Bon Jovi" shirt was because I really did love his music, not because my family was insanely poor.

This strategy worked until I stepped on the ice. I wasn't a very good skater at this time. All of my skating experience had been with white skates, and, as you can imagine, it's hard to learn something like skating when you're desperately hiding your face from certain embarrassment. Of course, as my "new" skates hit some of the boards, thanks to my lack of skill, the paint began to chip off.

Now, I'm no doctor, but I'm telling you, those kids must have had amazing eyesight, because they were able to spot a tiny speck or two of white from all the way across the rink. Cue the laughter and pointing. In that moment, no amount of Bon Jovi music could have helped me.

I thought I was going to die, but not only did I survive, I survived with a great story to tell.

This is when I learned my first life lesson.

Some of our best stories come from some of our worst experiences, so whenever I go through something rough, I try to think about it as a story I will tell one day. I learned at an early age to ask myself, "Is there something good, however small, that I can take from this bad?"

It's been said that the hardest struggle is the caterpillar's attempt to break free from its cocoon. If you saw this struggle, you might want to cut the cocoon to free the young butterfly. But if you did, the butterfly's wings wouldn't be strong enough and it wouldn't survive. Struggle is nature's way of preparing us for what's coming.

Pretty deep, eh? I got it from an episode of *Lost*, but if anyone asks, let's say it came to me on a mountaintop while I was helping a goat deliver its baby. Anyway, regardless of where it came from, it speaks to my first life lesson, that struggle doesn't have to be such a bad thing. Approaching life with this attitude can help us deal with many of the things that come our way. The idea is to find out what that good is and focus on it until we get through the bad.

So there I was, a very uncool young boy in elementary school with very little money, white skates and girly T-shirts. But I was also armed with my first life lesson, a boatload of good stories and a relatively positive attitude.

In addition to helping me have a good attitude, my first life lesson gave me an appreciation for life lessons in general and for tips of any kind. I was always on the lookout for how to do things better. If I saw someone getting into great shape, I was the first guy asking, "How did you do it?" If someone was really good at something I wanted to be good at, I hounded them for advice. I learned early on that the difference between winning and losing can come from the smallest of tips.

And that's what I'm here to explain to you through a series of stories, guidelines and strategies to make you better and to make your life easier. Consider this book your quick guide to being awesome at being awesome!

2

The Secret to Everything Awesome

AFTER I graduated from college my mother got pretty sick. She had cancer for eight years, and the chemo really took its toll. Eventually she was admitted to a department of the hospital where, unfortunately, patients don't leave because they've gotten better.

I was incredibly depressed during this time. I tried to channel my first life lesson and focus on the good, but I just couldn't see any. I had just landed my first office job and had started off well, but my work began to suffer because of my mother's situation, not to mention I was eating my feelings and getting incredibly fat. The extra weight was an extra problem I certainly didn't need.

One day my cousin came to visit my mom in the hospital. He had moved to New York a few years back and was kicking some serious butt in business. Thanks to my long-standing instinct of asking for advice, I mentioned I was on the verge of getting fired from my job and asked for any tips he might have.

He looked me up and down and said, "You're looking pretty out of shape. When was the last time you were in a gym?"

This, of course, insulted me and somewhat confused me, so I fired back at him. "What does that have to do with what I'm asking for? What does my being out of shape have to do with my job if I work in an office?"

My cousin went on to explain that it is all connected, that the way to happiness and success is through balancing body, mind and soul. He certainly didn't invent this way of thinking. Disciplines like Tai Chi and Yoga have promoted this for centuries. However, for many of us, the words "body, mind and soul" conjure up images of hippies sitting around and listening to music. Sounds like fun, but when it comes to a way of life, not realistic.

But let's step away from those images and look at things from a practical point of view. Think about the last time you were nervous about something and felt sick to your stomach. Something in your head made you physically ill. Now think about how good you felt after an empowering workout. Something in your body improved your mood. There is no denying the connection between our body, mind and soul.

The way my cousin looked at it, our body represents our health, strength and weight and how we feel about our appearance. Our mind represents things like our career, our finances and our education. Our soul represents everything else: our family, our relationships, our hobbies, our social life, our adventures, our charity, our connection to something spiritual.

Some people look at multiple successes in the same category and feel they have a balanced life. For example, they may say, "I have an expensive car, an expensive house, expensive clothes. Why do I feel like something is missing?" The reason is that their successes are all in the same category. There is no balance with anything else. How many times do we hear of someone who seemingly has it all but ends up incredibly depressed or even suicidal? We need to balance all the pieces that go into being human.

Sometimes we may want to intentionally unbalance ourselves. Maybe we just got a new job and need to spend most of our time on that, so we temporarily pull away from our family and other important things. Maybe a family member is sick, so we temporarily pull away from our jobs or school to take care of them. Or maybe we've gained a bunch of weight on vacation, so our main priority when we get back home is to lose that weight. It's okay to unbalance ourselves, as long as we know it's temporary and we're eventually going to balance things out again.

The bad news is that all it takes is for one of the categories of body, mind and soul to be off and it can drag the other two down. In my case, my mother's sickness was hurting my career and my health.

But the good news, as my cousin explained to me, is that success in one category can help pull the other two back up and help turn everything around.

That's why he asked me about the gym. When I told him work wasn't going well and I was on the verge of getting fired, he knew my "mind" category was not strong. With my mother being sick, he knew my "soul" category wasn't strong either. His goal was to give me success in the easiest category for me to fix at the time, the "body" category. He knew my family situation wasn't going to get better anytime soon, and I wasn't going to turn my career around in the next two weeks, but getting back in shape was something I could achieve in a short amount of time.

He knew that, by taking control of one-third of what makes me human, I would be in a better position to handle my career and to handle the inevitable death of my mother. That's not to say the death of a loved one will ever be easy, but if you're stronger in the other parts of your life, you'll fall apart that much less when something horrible happens. Sometimes that's the best we can do. Strengthen one aspect of your life, and it will help you strengthen the others. Take back one aspect of your life, and you can take them all back.

I have followed this practical approach to an ancient philosophy for the past fifteen years, and it has brought me back to awesome, picking me up from the worst time in my life. With it, I have achieved great success and overcome many obstacles, sometimes as a champion and sometimes just as someone who didn't completely fall apart when I otherwise could have.

This is something I believe in. It brings me success, peace, energy, happiness and overall awesomeness, and it can do so for you, too.

I have given many lectures on this subject. Every now and again someone questions my three categories. "Danny, I think there is more to us than just body, mind and soul," they say, going on to list a fourth category or even a fifth.

"It's not about the number," I say. "It's about balancing what's important to you. If you feel your life needs five categories, then work to balance all five."

For the purposes of this book, I work off of the body, mind and soul way of thinking.

And like my cousin suggested to me all those years ago, I want to start, in what follows, with the easiest part to fix: the body.

3

Achieving the Body You Want and Keeping It That Way

*F*OR my family, eating was like a religious experience.

We started our dinners with an appetizer, usually some sort of cured meat and cheese. This is where a lot of people made a mistake the first time they were invited over. They looked at this great spread and filled up on the appetizer. If they were still conscious after that, the actual meal was served, with numerous courses, all of which contained meat and all of which were designed for maximum fullness.

Our guests couldn't eat any more, but they'd have to, because my parents never took no for an answer when it came to eating.

The real fun began once dinner was over. We served pastries for dessert with, believe it or not, meat in them. Oh, and we brought out and served the original cured meat appetizer all over again.

Yes, my family loved meat, and they loved being full.

If dinner was over and you didn't need to be carried to the couch because your legs could no longer support your massive frame, then something was wrong.

My parents would look at abstaining guests and say, "Whatsa matter, you no like?"

The guests would try to explain by saying, "No, no, everything is great – I just can't eat any more or I'll explode."

Mom and Dad's only suggestion, of course, was to eat some more.

That was my family's answer to every problem, kind of our all-purpose Plan B. You lose your job? Eat something. A death in the family? Eat something. Time to celebrate? Eat something. Anything that happened, good or bad – you guessed it, eat something. Gluttony was, and still is, my family's favorite sport.

That being said, given how obesity levels have been on the rise for some time now, gluttony must be a lot of people's favorite sport. We've all heard the stories and seen the facts about the many health issues associated with excess weight, and of course we feel bad when we're going through a period of weight gain. But, as my cousin taught me, the problem goes beyond our body and how we feel about it. Our weight and our control of it are connected to so much more.

A colleague always complained to me about his weight. For years he told me how he hated being fat. He figured he was about 100 pounds overweight. This colleague also always complained about feeling stuck in his career.

I told him I felt his two problems were connected. I went on to explain my body, mind and soul theory and offered to help him lose weight. I put him on a weight-loss plan. In what seemed like a very short time, he dropped 50 pounds. He had more energy and confidence than he'd had in years. This gave him an incredibly positive attitude and helped him make immediate positive changes in his career. Taking back one aspect of his life helped him take back the rest.

When dealing with weight issues, nothing is more important than balance. Lots of information in the media about losing weight can be confusing, but it all breaks down to a very simple formula: striking a healthy balance between the calories that go in our bodies and the calories that go out. That's it. That's all that matters. All weight loss and weight gain comes from this. If we take in more calories than we burn, we'll gain weight. If we burn more calories than we take in, we'll lose weight.

John Cisna, a high school science teacher from Colo, Iowa, ate nothing but McDonald's for 90 days. The result? He lost weight!

His approach was the opposite of filmmaker Morgan Spurlock's in the Oscar-nominated documentary *Super Size Me*. Spurlock ate nothing but McDonald's for 30 days to demonstrate how negatively fast food can impact one's body. He gained 24.5 pounds, and his cholesterol shot up by 65 points.

Cisna wanted to prove that, with a smart calorie plan, it's possible to lose weight even if you eat fast food for every meal. His diet was so successful, he lost 60 pounds in three months. And his meals didn't just include salads and fruit parfaits. He ate Big Macs and similar sandwiches, too. In addition to losing weight, his cholesterol level improved.

He was able to accomplish this by sticking to a calorie-specific diet and by following the Food and Drug Administration's nutrition guidelines. In addition to calorie counting, he also walked briskly four or five times a week for 45 minutes.

I have dropped weight and have helped numerous people lose weight – up to 100 pounds – in the same manner as Cisna (but without becoming a fixture at McDonald's). The first thing you need to do is find out the number of calories you can take in daily in order to lose two pounds a week. I like the two-pounds-a-week goal because it's realistic, manageable and simple, so you're less likely to cheat. Also, you'll be less likely to be left with the flab that comes with rapid weight loss. Take your time, go slow and you'll have a tight body as you transition.

Some may disagree with this strategy. If they don't drop weight quickly, they quit their diets. That being said, if two pounds is not right for you, you still need to find a realistic and healthy number that fits your life-style and personality.

Here's the best part: once you find out the daily caloric number that will get you to your weekly weight-loss goal, you can take those calories from whatever food you want. So nutrients aside and speaking strictly from a weight-loss point of view, if my goal is 2,000 calories a day, then I can eat 2,000 calories worth of chocolate and still lose weight. Of course, I wouldn't recommend this, for a slew of health reasons.

As for the age-old debate about whether all calo-ries are the same, the answer is yes and no. How's that for clarity? What I mean is that, when it comes to the math of weight loss, 2,000 calories from chocolate are the same as 2,000 calories from apples. However, just like there are good fats and bad fats, good carbs and bad carbs, there are of course good calories and bad calories. If we eat nothing but junk and processed foods but stay within our daily caloric limit, we'll lose weight, but we'll be incredibly unhealthy. A calorie may be a calorie on paper, but we still need to take in quality foods with essential nutrients, just as John Cisna did despite his McDonald's-only diet.

Many who have taken my weight-loss advice take in most of their allotted calories from a healthy balance of things that are good for the body, like non-processed whole foods consisting of healthy fats, veggies, proteins, carbs and so on. Then, for about 10% of their allocated daily calories, they splurge on some good-for-the-soul junk food. I've had people lose more than 50 pounds following this method. They never felt they were on a diet because of that little bit of junk food every day, so they never felt the need to cheat or binge.

That's what I love about calorie counting: I don't need to cut anything out of my diet. As long as I stay within my daily calories, I can have my carbs, I can have my fats and I can eat before bed. I can even have a little bit of junk food every day. Anytime I've ever cut anything out of my diet, it always made its way back with a vengeance. That's why I don't like diets that allow for a weekly cheat day. At first these diets seemed great, but they just ended up making me feel sick and I couldn't turn off that part of my brain the next day. My cheat day would turn into a cheat weekend and then a cheat week and eventually a cheat month.

If you strike a daily balance of the things you like, including junk food, you won't need to go nuts on any particular day. It's not just about reaching a goal but about learning a healthy, easy-to-adopt lifestyle you can maintain forever.

Naturally, this may lead you to wonder how to determine your ideal caloric number while including healthy fats, carbs and proteins in your diet. There are a lot of free websites and mobile apps that break this information down easily to help you track your progress. The key to any of these programs is honesty. If you're a couch potato, that's okay – just say you are. The more accurate you are when working with these sites and apps, the more accurate your plan will be.

You can find the caloric amount and nutrient information online for almost any food you can think of. You can even find information for restaurant menus. Look for a site that comes highly recommended. (For sites and apps I really like, see the resources list at the end of this book. Additionally, I keep an updated list on my website, www.AwesomeAtBeingAwesome.com.)

Ideally, you want a site that's free and has a large database of the foods you eat and the activities you participate in. Look for one that can tell you specifically how many calories you can consume daily to lose two pounds a week based on your goals and current lifestyle and that can help you track your progress.

Once you understand your daily caloric limit, you can plan your meals, which will make you less likely to cheat. The very act of tracking calories will help you with weight loss. When you see on paper exactly what you're eating, it's easier to cut out what you don't need.

As you get comfortable with your daily limit, you can start to play around with different foods and really maximize your enjoyment of those calories. If your limit is 1,500 a day, instead of blowing the whole 1,500 on one hamburger, look for a substitute to that hamburger that satisfies your craving but takes up fewer calories. This will allow you to enjoy your calories much more.

The same goes for cheat calories. If you're going to spend 200 calories eating a chocolate bar, look around for ones that give you the most flavor and grams for the least amount of calories. There are a lot of healthy and tasty low-calorie products out there that will leave you feeling full. Take your time and experiment with different foods until you find what you love. For some great low-calorie treats and meal ideas, visit www. AwesomeAtBeingAwesome.com.

As you start playing with the numbers on the calorie sites and apps, you'll notice that, as you increase your physical activities, you can increase the amount of calories allotted to you. This makes sense because it brings us back to calories in versus calories out.

There are a bunch of options available for picking the physical activity that's right for you. A lot of great videos make it easy for you to work out at home. You put them on and follow the program and don't need to think much more about it. For those who prefer to get out of the house, the gym is a great option. You want to do a mix of cardio and weight lifting, but, most importantly, track your activities along with your calories because, as any body builder will tell you, 80 percent of the effort put in to your body should come from the kitchen and not the gym. Understanding the daily caloric number that will get you to your goal and sticking to that number is far more important than exercise.

You may be like many who find the idea of counting calories painful. In the past it was, but today the new sites and apps do the thinking for you. That being said, if you still don't like the idea of counting calories, there's no shortage of companies that will be happy to take your money and do it for you. Ultimately, you need to go with what works for you. However, with a little bit of effort you can save yourself a bunch of money, not to mention you'll be learning how to control your eating on your own. If you pay someone to do the work for you, you'll just put all the weight back on once you stop paying them.

By understanding the way calories work and using the means described in this chapter to strike a healthy balance between the calories in and calories out, you'll never have a problem with weight again. With a healthy, confident and balanced body, you'll be in a better position to strengthen and balance your mind and soul.

4

Introducing the ABCs of Life

*I*N the previous chapter I gave you some practical advice regarding the body. The next three chapters also deal with good physical health but focus on the mind and soul.

When talking about the mind and soul, I've noticed that the characteristics and tips I've used to bring me great success in my career, education and finances also seem to work really well with my family, marriage, friends and personal life. I follow a very simple formula that I call Danny's ABCs of Life. The letters stand for:

Attitude
Basics
Communication

I've often felt I was very average. I've never been the most athletic, certainly never the most popular, never the smartest, never the most creative and...well, you get the point: never the greatest at anything. Many people, and I'm not just referring to bullies, told me repeatedly that I was actually well below average in many things. Friends told me, teachers told me, and even my parents told me, usually on the topic of my room-cleaning abilities, but still, in many aspects of life, I was and am a very average, sometimes even slightly below average person.

You may feel this about yourself, even just some of the time, and that's okay, because the great thing about this ABC formula is that, by following it, you can go from being average or even slightly below average to not just being awesome but being awesome at being awesome.

To show you what I mean, take a look at the formula from the point of view of being well above average in many things but lacking in the three simple traits of the ABC formula.

You can be the smartest person in the world, but if you have a terrible **attitude** that causes people to not like you, life will be very hard on you.

You can have all the contacts in the world, but if you don't follow the **basics** and give people what you promised within the time frame promised, no one will want to work with you because they will feel they can't rely on you.

And you can have the greatest idea in the world, but if you can't **communicate** it to others in a way that gets them to listen to you, your idea will do you very little good.

However, if you excel at the ABCs and people love your attitude and feel they can rely on you because you're good at the basics and they love listening to you communicate, then you will do great things – even if you're not the smartest person in the room, even if you have no contacts and even if your idea is not the greatest.

In short, people want to work with, do business with and have relationships with people they like, people they can rely on and people they like conversing with. Focus on mastering the ABCs and you will achieve incredible success and happiness.

Read on for a breakdown of each component of my ABCs, starting in the next chapter with the first and most often overlooked component: attitude.

5

The Right ATTITUDE for Your Body, Mind and Soul

*I*T has been proven that negative emotions can cause sickness. Stress can completely break the body down; a panic attack can feel very much like a heart attack and do incredible damage.

It has also been proven that every action has an equal and opposite reaction. If negative emotion can make us sick, then positive emotion can make us healthy. A positive attitude can change our life, can change the lives of others around us and can change the world.

That being said, how do we remain positive in a world filled with so much negativity?

As I mentioned in chapter 1 about my first life lesson, when I'm faced with an obstacle I try to see if I can take anything good from it. As a kid, I learned that bad days sometimes make for good stories. As an adult, I learned that problems can often lead to opportunity.

Psychologist Walter Mischel led a series of studies at Stanford University in the 1960s in which children were given a marshmallow but told they could have it and another marshmallow if they waited 15 minutes to eat it. Many years later, a follow-up study revealed that the children who were able to wait for that second marshmallow had a better life in terms of academic results, body weight and income. These were the kids who saw past the problem of waiting the 15 minutes and focused on the positive opportunity of two marshmallows.

Thinking this way can be difficult because we live in a time of instant gratification. The world wants us to be comfortable and not wait around for that second marshmallow.

This study really spoke to me because, time and time again, I have experienced the practical advantage of focusing on the opportunity instead of the problem.

For example, if you're the kind of worker who complains about where you work, you probably have a long list of everything you hate about your company. But let's say you could wave a magic wand and make the company you work for perfect. Would that make you happy? It most certainly would not. Why? Because in a perfect company, there's no reason to change anything and therefore no room for opportunity. You'd better be happy with the job you have and the money you make because in a perfect company you're never going to be promoted. Why would there need to be promotions when everything is perfect?

One of the biggest and best moves I made in my career was based not on the positive traits of the company where I was working at the time but on the problems and obstacles it was facing. The company employed a lot of smart engineers who came up with amazing solutions but were very bad at explaining what they did. I knew I could use my love of explaining things to help the company, not to mention my own career. While everyone else was looking for the "perfect company," I was looking for the "perfect set of problems" for my skill set that would allow me to make a name for myself. Spotting the opportunity within a problem was a strategy I implemented early on in my career. It has brought me success ever since.

At another point in my career, I was in sales and was getting set to take on my first big account, or, as we called it, "enterprise account." Big problem, though: the company I worked for was suing the company behind this enterprise account. Pretty hard to sell to a company you're suing, right?

A few of my colleagues cracked jokes about my situation, and most of my friends told me I should have refused the account. But I didn't see it as a problem. I was actually glad there was a lawsuit. I was still fairly junior in the company. I knew I would never have been given such a big account unless a big problem was attached to it. Basically, I got it because no one else wanted it. I saw an opportunity where everyone else saw a problem. I figured I just had to be patient. Once the lawsuit went away, I'd be the one left with this fantastic account.

And that's exactly what happened. The account ended up being the biggest our team had ever seen. Even better, I put a sizable down payment on my first home with the commission I generated from that account.

At yet another point in my career, my boss had quit. I decided to step up and ask for the job. Many of my colleagues and friends said I was crazy for wanting to take over a team that was in such bad shape. But once again, I saw the opportunity, not the problem. The opportunity was mine only because the team was in bad shape and no one else wanted it. I knew I'd be a hero if I could turn it around. Not to mention, getting into management could be a career game changer for me. If I couldn't turn the team around, at the very least I'd have a management job title on my résumé. The move definitely worked to my advantage.

A positive attitude not only will teach you how to pick the right opportunities by seeing past a problem; it will also ensure that more opportunities present themselves to you.

There was a time in my career when I was conducting interviews to fill a data-entry position on our team. Some of the people who came in for the interview had horrible attitudes and looked like they really didn't want to be there.

Then this one guy came in, perhaps the least qualified of the bunch, and said to me, "I want this job so bad, I'll even sweep the floors on my downtime. I'll be the best employee you've ever had!"

I was so blown away by his positive, dedicated attitude that I hired him on the spot. He turned out to be amazing.

The fact is, a skill will always improve with time, but a bad attitude will just keep getting worse.

My nephew complained to me once that his teacher gave him a bad grade because she didn't like him. It wasn't fair, he said, because his grades should be based on his work not his poor behavior. When I asked him why his teacher didn't like him, he said it was because he was always causing trouble.

"This is one of the most important life lessons you could ever learn," I said. "When you're a kid and a teacher doesn't like you, it may result in a bad grade. But when you're an adult and a leader doesn't like you, it could mean not getting a promotion or not getting a job. It could even result in getting you fired."

At the end of the day, we are all human, even the most powerful executives among us. All we really want to do is work with people we like. Having a positive attitude is the foundation of being someone people like.

One thing that helps me remain positive is sharing my positivity. For example, I used to go to the same takeout restaurant every day for lunch and order the same thing, a chicken wrap. Slowly but surely the lady who served me kept increasing the amount of chicken in my wrap. I knew she wasn't doing it to earn a tip because she didn't work the cash register and there was no tip jar in sight.

Eventually I asked her, "Why are you so nice to me?"

"Because I work very long hours," she said, "and you're the only person who smiles at me and asks me how my day is going."

This woman served so many people who were rude to her or just plain oblivious of her that she had come to appreciate simple common courtesy and felt the need to thank me for it with an extra stuffed wrap. This is when I realized that positivity breeds more positivity.

Another time I was at the dentist's office for a check-up after I'd had my wisdom teeth removed. I told the dentist I thought he and his team were extremely professional and I was amazed by how well the experience went. You should have seen this guy's smile. He couldn't contain himself. He went on to tell me no one complimented him in his line of work and I had made his day.

As I was leaving, I was preparing to pay the $100 check-up fee, but the dentist came out to thank me again for making his day and said there would be no charge. I saved $100 just by complimenting this man! But more important than the money was how good this man's positive reaction made me feel.

On vacation a few years ago, my wife and I were at a restaurant with a good friend. We were having a great time. When the owner of the restaurant came by to check on us, I told her that my wife and I had been traveling for two weeks, and that her restaurant was by far my favorite. My wife would argue that, when I'm in a good mood, everything is my favorite, but, either way, in that moment, everything was perfect, and to me it was the best restaurant I had ever been in and I felt the owner should know. The owner was extremely pleased with my comment and told me that I had really made her day.

At the end of the meal, I asked the server for the bill, but instead he came back with the owner, who said there would be no charge. I should point out this was not a small meal. It consisted of appetizers, a main course, dessert and, of course, lots of wine, and all for three people. I wasn't about to let anyone pay for such an expensive meal on our behalf, but the owner insisted, saying the cost was nothing compared with how good I had made her feel.

I didn't argue any further. I thanked her for her wonderful treatment and left a tip for the server. Later, as we walked through the streets of that town, we discussed what a great night we'd had and the fact it was all paid for. But for me, the best part was what that owner said to me. Knowing I was responsible for making someone feel that good made me feel amazing!

My favorite story of sharing positive energy happened in connection with my weekly runs to the grocery store. When I was paying my bill on one of these occasions, the young cashier handed me a note and asked me to read it when I left the store.

The note said that four weeks earlier she had wanted to kill herself. Things in her life were completely out of hand. She had recently announced to her family and friends that she was gay and it had not gone well. They weren't accepting of it, and things had gotten so bad she couldn't take it any longer. So she woke up one day and decided to go to work so she could talk to one of her friends one last time. After finishing her shift, she was going to kill herself.

When I came to her cash register that very day, she wrote, I had noted it wasn't very busy in the store and had said, "I always know it's going to be a good day when there's no line-up."

"I guess it doesn't take much for you to have a good day, then," she replied.

"That's because I'm always looking for an excuse to have a good day."

Her note went on to explain how I had made her laugh, and she had told herself our conversation was going to be her excuse for having a good day and her reason for not killing herself that day. The next day she found another excuse, and the day after that, another one. This went on for five days until she realized she didn't want to die and needed therapy. She credited me for saving her life.

Although I certainly can't take any credit for the incredible strength this young lady displayed, I'm always reminded when I think of her that we live our life one day at a time and have the amazing power to make or break someone else's day with just a few words. What kind of person do you want to be? Do you want to be the kind of person who breaks people down or who builds them up?

I could tell you many more stories about how good it feels to display a positive attitude. I put positive energy out there and it so often comes right back to me, which only puts me in an even better mood. I've never understood how people can be mad at one person and take it out on another. When I'm mad at one person, I'm happy to be dealing with another because it means I'm no longer dealing with the person who initially upset me. When something bad happens at work, I'm happy to get home, because at least I'm no longer in the place that frustrated me. I carry my positive attitude everywhere, and always leave the negative behind.

Remaining positive can be harder some days than others, especially when we're met with a slew of negativity.

When I was younger, I loved martial arts. I loved watching old Bruce Lee movies on TV. My parents didn't have enough money for lessons, but that didn't stop me from practicing around the house. I copied moves from TV, from books, from anything I could get my hands on.

When my family and friends saw me doing this, they laughed and said I was crazy for attempting to learn something as complicated as martial arts without proper training and coaching. "Why are you even bothering with this?" they often asked me.

But I never let their negativity stop me. The way I looked at it, a long time ago somebody must have done this without the benefit of a trainer. Who trained the first martial artist? If that guy could do it, so could I.

I ended up being really good at it. As my skills took shape, my friends and family stopped asking me *why* I was doing it and started asking me *how* I was doing it.

Don't let someone's negativity stop you from at least trying; after all, so many great accomplishments start off as crazy ideas.

So let's recap. A positive attitude is extremely important to your career, your personal life, even your health. Being positive means seeing that many problems are opportunities in disguise and some crazy ideas are really the early stages of greatness.

You can maintain a positive attitude by putting it out there and receiving positive energy back. It's like what our mothers taught us when they sent us to school: be nice to the other kids and they'll be nice to you. We can do this with simple things like smiling at people and, of course, saying please and thank you. They really are magic words.

Lastly, when people do something you like, tell them. Why are we so afraid to compliment people? As long as we mean it and as long as it's appropriate, we should never be afraid to give a compliment.

Having a good life starts with having a good day, so the next time you're feeling bad and think you have no control over your life, remember, you have the amazing power to completely make someone else's day with just a few small words. In doing so, their positive reaction may make your day. All of this is in your power because you are awesome!

6

The BASICS of Being Awesome at Work and at Home

*A*s mentioned earlier, I grew up poor. Not having a lot of material things can help you appreciate the finer things in life. But sometimes you just don't want to wear your sister's Bon Jovi T-shirts anymore. To move on from anything like that fashion nightmare and to make your days a bit easier, you need a little bit of spending cash. Whether it be a part-time job or a career, employment becomes a necessary part of life.

I remember my first job in great detail. My dad would drive me to work, saying, "Come on, let's go to Cracker Cheese." You've probably never heard of Cracker Cheese, and that's because the real name of this place is Chuck E. Cheese's, but for some reason my dad could never say that. He called it Cracker Cheese, Chicken Cheese, he even called it Cream Cheese, but never Chuck E. Cheese's.

Whatever you call it, it's a place where a kid can be a kid. Unfortunately, I never went there as a kid. I only went as a teenager, and only to work.

I was the Chuck E. Cheese mascot. My job was to walk around patting kids on the head while they took out their aggressions by kicking me. If those kids came to Chuck E. Cheese's angry, they certainly went home happy. That essentially was my job: to walk around and take a beating from children. It didn't bother me too much. I'd taken beatings before. At least now I was getting paid for it.

I was well liked by the managers because of my good attitude about the beatings, so they quickly promoted me to the kitchen, and I started making pizzas. The good news: more money, and no more beatings from kids. The bad news: this job was way more complicated, and I was terrible at making pizza. I thought I was going to get fired. This is where I thought my positive, friendly attitude had backfired: it had handed me an opportunity I clearly wasn't ready for. Because I got this new job based on personality and not skill, fear set in. *I got the job, now what? I don't know what I'm doing.*

But I ended up learning something in that kitchen I've been following ever since. To excel at any task, even very complicated ones, you need to follow the basics.

The first thing I noticed about the world of pizza-making was that all new employees had something in common: their first few pizzas always sucked. Even if someone had made pizza at home a million times, their skills never translated well in a really big kitchen. We made them slowly, and they looked ugly. But eventually, our skills improved until we became pizza-making ninja masters, quickly creating pizzas that looked and tasted great.

This showed me that, as mentioned in the previous

chapter, a skill will always improve with time. And, as also mentioned in the previous chapter, a bad attitude will only get worse.

Sometimes a bad attitude has to do with personality. Sometimes it has to do with an inability to follow the basics.

I noticed the guys who came to work late and cut corners got worse in those behaviors the longer they were employed. Their pizza-making skills improved, but that didn't matter because they were unreliable. Yes, they were good while they were there, many of them better than I was, but there was no guarantee of when they would get to work, if they showed up at all. Of course this behavior inevitably got them fired no matter how good their skills were.

Eventually I was promoted to team lead of that kitchen. That was the first of many promotions in my life. I got it not because I had the best pizza skills on the team but because I was the most reliable. Too many people spend their time worrying about being great at great things and forget about being great at little things – the basics, like showing up on time.

I remember conducting a conference call at a later job. Two engineers from my company were on the call and five engineers from the client's side. Eight people in total, with only one of them unable to understand anything that anyone was saying. That would be me. The conversation was so technical, I was lost within five seconds.

At first I thought I should start looking for another job because I was way out of my league. But I kept telling myself not to worry about it and to just focus on the basics. Just run the call.

I took down everyone's name at the start of the call. I recapped my understanding of why we were meeting. Then I asked people to add their thoughts. When it was coming to an end, I asked if everyone was satisfied with the discussion and clear on the next steps. I confirmed that I would send out an email recapping the discussion points and next steps.

As I hung up the phone, my fears kicked in again, and I thought maybe this wasn't the right job for me. The technology was just too complicated for me to understand. But then the client called to thank me for running such an efficient call. "I've never been on a call with that many engineers that went so smoothly," she said.

That completely made my day. It made me realize that, whether the job is making pizzas or speaking with scary smart engineers, there needs to be someone everyone can rely on, someone who focuses on the basics.

It seems the world is so fast-paced, many people are forgetting the basics. Technology can help us do things we weren't able to do before, but it can't provide common courtesy or professionalism. People miss deadlines, show up late for meetings and don't call you back when they say they will. This behavior happens so often that it's becoming generally accepted. The bar has been lowered so much that, if you do these very basic things properly, you'll be considered a leader just for doing your job.

After my sister took time off to raise her three kids, she was ready to get back into the workforce. When she got her first job, she asked me for some advice. I gave her my usual speech on the importance of the basics. During her first week on the job, her team was asked to fill out a document and submit it before the next team meeting. My sister did what was asked of her within the time frame requested. When she submitted her document, her boss raved about her, calling her a leader and telling her she would go far in the organization. My sister was puzzled as to why her boss was so happy with her for simply doing what was asked. Eventually, she found out no one else had completed the assignment. She was a leader simply for following the basics.

A mechanic friend of mine told me about a new young employee at his garage. This new guy had high hopes. He was always talking about his dream to be the greatest mechanic of all time. But he was always late and always cut corners. One day he didn't put all the necessary locks in place and a car fell off a hoist and was destroyed, a very expensive mistake. It could have been so much worse; luckily, no one was hurt. Either way, the new guy was fired on the spot, and word of his reputation got out to other garages. Soon no one wanted to hire him. It got so bad he left the industry and went into something completely different. The really sad part is he had all of the necessary skills to be a master mechanic. His down-fall was his inability to follow the basics.

Another friend of mine is always hiring contractors to work around his home. He told me how, by doing this, he has gotten to know how different companies work – which have the best-skilled workers, which have better prices and which are more reliable and actually call you back and have workers who show up when they're supposed to.

I was at his house one night and asked him, "What

makes you decide to give repeat business to a contractor? Do you lean more towards price or skill?"

Those were important pieces of the decision, he told me, but number one was reliability. "If a contractor is consistently late," he said, "I know he has no respect for the basics. Even if he has the better skill and price, I know his sloppiness in work practices will result in some sloppiness in the work itself."

I've known multiple salespeople throughout my career who had amazing skills. They were friendly, charming and incredibly smart, and they were amazing presenters, but they didn't follow the basics. They didn't make the necessary sales calls, they didn't do their research, and they didn't honor time commitments. Their amazing skill set did not save them from inevitable failure. It doesn't matter how smart and talented you are, if you can't follow the basics and be relied on, you will never be a leader, and you will never be awesome.

When I managed a team at one point in my career, I was always shocked by how many people missed deadlines they themselves had set and agreed to. After a deadline passed, I would call them to ask for whatever report I needed and was barraged with a slew of excuses. I never accepted any of the excuses, not because I was unreasonable, not because I really needed what they were supposed to do by a certain time, but because we had an agreement, and I was hearing the excuses only after the deadline had passed.

If I had gotten a call even five minutes before the deadline explaining the situation, what was being done about it and what the new deadline was, it would have been more understandable and manageable. I'm not saying all projects have to be completed. Sometimes, for whatever reason, we're given a task that simply can't be done. But it's up to us to make that known as soon as we see a problem.

The same rules apply in our personal lives. How many times do we hear about problems between friends or family members simply because someone didn't do something they said they would do? This seems to be a root cause of so many recurring fights between parents and their children, between spouses and between friends. How many times have we heard or told someone, "You said you were going to take out the garbage," "You said you were going to clean your room," or "You said you were going to call me"? Whether we're talking about a big corporation or a family member, nobody likes to be misled, and nobody likes someone they can't rely on.

One of the greatest tools you can use to your advantage professionally is your calendar. Without one, it's not possible for you to remember all the deadlines you need to meet or all the calls you need to make. The minute you have a project, designate a spot on your calendar when you know you can work on it; then you don't need to think about it or worry about it again until it's time to do so. When the time comes, complete the task as planned and promised. Likewise, if you need information from someone and they say they'll get back to you, put a reminder in your calendar to follow up with that person.

You can even do this in your personal life. I have an aunt who always got mad at me because I kept forgetting to call her. I finally started taking my own advice and put a reminder in my calendar. It was one of the greatest things I've ever done for our relationship. I do this with friends' birthdays, too, and I even leave myself reminders if someone is starting a new job and I want to send them a nice note on their first day.

Not unlike the benefits of tracking your calories, as discussed in chapter 3, tracking your obligations will help you meet your goals. It'll also relieve a lot of stress, for three main reasons.

First, you'll be less likely to miss deadlines or important dates because you won't be caught off guard.

Second, you'll get into far fewer confrontations with colleagues or loved ones because you won't be missing deadlines or important dates.

Third, you won't need to worry about projects or special events until the allotted times in your calendar.

We spend so much time worrying about being great at great things. But to be great at great things, or awesome at being awesome, for that matter, we first need to be awesome at the basics. Learn to excel at the basics, and you will excel in your career, as well as in your personal life.

Here are four great tips to help you strengthen relationships with your boss, co-workers, family and friends:

1. **Show up on time**. Whether it's a business meeting or a get-together with friends, when you're late, you're saying, "My time is more important than your time." It's a sign of disrespect.

2. **Show up prepared**. Sometimes taking 10 minutes before a meeting to look over your notes can make all the difference in the world.

3. **Be accountable**. Do what you say you're going to do within the time frame you agreed to or give a reason why it can't be done. If something changes and a deadline can no longer be met, reset expectations as soon as possible. Don't wait for the deadline to pass.

4. **Use your calendar to your advantage in both your professional and personal life**.

I actually honed my skill at the basics as a kid at Halloween each year. Everyone loved Halloween when they were young. Who am I kidding? I still do. But when I was a kid, it was different. To me and my friends, Halloween wasn't about fun or costumes or playing around. It was about one thing and one thing only: free candy. It was the one night of the year when all kids were created equal. Candy was out there waiting for everyone. It didn't matter how much money your parents had, because the candy was all free. The only thing that mattered was how many houses you could hit on that one magical night, and we were ready to hit as many as physically possible.

So we trained for Halloween the way athletes train for the Olympics. While other kids were busy doing whatever it was kids did, we were busy planning a strategy for maximum neighborhood candy-grabbing.

Back in the day, parents didn't really go out with the kids to trick or treat, at least not our parents. Because of that, there was always the danger of older kids roaming the streets to take your candy. So in addition to planning the best street routes, we planned for candy muggers. Our tactics were to stay in well-lit areas, always be on the lookout for danger and have safe houses for shelter if we ran into trouble.

Our plans were very basic but very effective. In all of those years, no one collected as much candy as we did. And as many times as would-be candy thieves tried to steal from us, no one ever succeeded.

The fact is, whether you're trying to conquer life, conquer a career, make a pizza or get your hands on as much Halloween candy as possible, respect for and mastery of the basics is your path to awesomeness.

And by mastering the basics, it'll be much easier for you to have a positive attitude. Both attitude and the basics tie in to the final piece of my ABCs of Life: communication.

7

Awesome COMMUNICATION at Work and at Home

*I*N elementary school, kids teased me all the time. They poked fun at me for all kinds of things. Then one day, that began to change.

I was in sixth grade and was on lunch break, sitting at my desk eating my sandwich. At one point, the teacher stepped out of the room, and one of the kids got up and walked towards me. I could tell by the way my classmates reacted that he was coming over to make fun of me.

"Just keep your head down and keep quiet," I said to myself, "and eventually this guy will go away."

As I sat there, hoping not to be noticed, the boy said, "Nice pants, Danny. I would have bought the same pair, but my penny rolled down the sewer."

Back in my day, this was known as a "burn." Kids tormented each other with these insults and everyone would laugh.

"It's okay, Danny. Just keep quiet, and he'll go away," I told myself. But instead, without even thinking, I said, "Why should it be a problem that your penny rolled down the sewer? Isn't that where your family lives?"

Not only did I stun the boy and the class, but I stunned myself as well. "Where the hell did that come from?" I asked myself. I generally was friendly. Maybe I always had something I wanted to say, but when you go to school wearing your sister's outfits, you keep a low profile. I had no idea I could communicate so effectively.

The whole class exploded with laughter, and the would-be bully was reduced to shreds. It didn't matter that I wasn't popular. It didn't matter that I was coming from a position of weakness. All that mattered was knowing what to say. From that day forward, whether I was wearing girly T-shirts or the whitest skates on the planet, I knew elementary school – and the rest of the world, for that matter – would be a lot less scary as long as I communicated well.

The ability to communicate is one of the most powerful and useful tools in our kit as we make the transition from average to awesome. You may have the greatest idea in the world, but if you can't explain it in a way that persuades people to listen to you, your idea will do you little good. You may be the most qualified job applicant on the planet, but if you can't communicate well enough to get past the interview, you will not get the job. It doesn't matter how smart you are or how good your ideas are if you can't get anyone to listen to you.

By the same token, you could be coming from a position of terrible weakness, like wearing your sister's

T-shirts, but if you know what to say, and can say it so everyone is compelled to listen to you, you have real power.

People struggle with public speaking and communication in general. If you're good at it, you have an automatic advantage over many others.

One of the main reasons people are generally bad at public speaking is fear. In one of his jokes, Jerry Seinfeld refers to a statistic that reveals a majority of people fear public speaking more than death. As Seinfeld points out, this means most people at a funeral would rather be the guy in the casket than the guy delivering the eulogy.

To understand why public speaking or communicating in general is so scary for so many people, let's start by breaking down what's involved in effective communication. Essentially, there are two main elements to a speech or any other kind of presentation: the message and the delivery. We need to think of what we are going to say (the message) and how we're going to say it (the delivery).

Whether it's giving a speech, being interviewed for a job or breaking bad news to the boss, it's usually the delivery part that makes us most nervous. But that is a misplaced fear, because the reason the delivery is so scary is that we're not comfortable with the message itself. That's where the real problem lies. Many of us aren't sure of what we're going to say, the order we're going to say it in or what our actual point is, so of course we get nervous when we need to speak.

On the flip side, think about the last time someone asked you to speak about something you know really well and are passionate about – maybe your hobby or a vacation you just took or what you did on the weekend. As you told your story, others gathered around to listen. There you were, with no time to prepare for this presentation and no training in public speaking, telling a story with ease and confidence to a small crowd.

How did that happen? Because you were comfortable with your message.

Understand your message, master your message and the delivery will come more easily.

Although the message and the delivery are the two main elements of preparing a speech, a lot of people will unnecessarily and unwisely spend much of their time on a third category: visual aids. They put hours in to these and only minutes in to what they're going to say and how they're going to say it. But visual aids are meant to be just that: something that *aids* your message. The message itself must be your focus.

Think about it. Have you ever heard anyone say, "I didn't like the speaker, but wow, those slides were great"? No matter how nice they look, visual aids will not hold your audience's attention – only your message will. And here's an extra tip: If your message does require a visual aid, don't include a lot of text in it. Your audience is not going to read long paragraphs off a slide. Instead, use charts, pictures or quotes that back up your message.

Some people place too much importance on other minor elements of a speech like body language or the tone and pitch of their voice. Only when it comes to things like flirting is body language more powerful than what you're actually saying verbally. I'll never forget the first time a girl touched my arm. I gotta tell you, as you may have guessed from reading about my childhood, it didn't happen to me a lot growing up, so when it did, it was a big deal. We were talking, she was laughing and then she reached out and touched my arm.

I'm pretty sure I went deaf after that because I didn't hear a word she said for the rest of the conversation. But even though I couldn't hear her, she had me hanging on to her every word. It was such a powerful experience that, many years later, I married her, but that's another story. The point is, in every other case, body language is of minor importance compared with your actual message.

The same may be said about the tone of your voice. A lot of people disagree with me on this, but if the tone of a speaker's voice is so important, why is Stephen Hawking so captivating? When we listen to him, we're hearing a computerized voice, yet we're still amazed by his brilliant message.

So, at least for now, forget about visual aids, forget about body language, forget about tone and your voice and focus on your message. If you master the message, all of the other pieces will start to fall into place. The world will become less scary, and you'll start to feel a greater confidence in your speaking as well as other aspects of your life.

Some people are naturals at creating messages. They easily launch into an entertaining presentation or story. However, if, as part of your educational or professional duties, you need to be consistently effective several times a week or even several times a day, being a natural communicator is not enough. If you rely on natural talent, your performance will vary depending on how you feel that day.

I knew that, if I wanted to make a living out of communicating with people, I needed to be good all the time. So I analyzed what I did when I was at my best. When I delivered a speech or a message of some kind and it felt like everything coming out of my mouth was perfect, what was I doing? Why was I good some days and bad other days? Eventually I came up with a formula that helps me get the perfect message out every time.

Whether you're born with the gift of gab or you hate public speaking, a formula like mine will help *you* communicate effectively every time. Of course practicing or rehearsing a speech is an obvious way to improve. However, not everything can be rehearsed. What if you get asked a difficult question and need to answer right away? Rehearsing won't help you with that, but if you understand the mechanics of how to craft a great message, you can sound good all the time, even when coming from a position of weakness or having a lack of prep time.

I like to start my message formula with an audience welcome. I usually start with my name. It's amazing to me how many people give presentations without saying their name. I also mention my relevance to the topic. If I'm leading a seminar on effective communication, I may say something like, "Hi, my name is Danny Pehar, and public speaking is a big part of my life." By doing this, I let the audience know who I am and give them a reason to listen to me. I may also go over any logistics. For example, if I'm the meeting's chairperson, I may tell them where the washrooms are located, how to go about asking a question, things like that.

Then I clearly state my topic: "I'm here today to talk

to you about effective communication." In addition to not mentioning their name, most people don't mention their topic, leaving the audience confused before anything's even started.

These first steps may seem very simple, but it's the little things that cause audience members to like you and not even realize *why* they like you. It's about making it easier on your audience to listen to you. A clear, concise welcome and topic statement allows you to organize your thoughts, and it also allows your audience to warm up to you.

Now that you've got the welcome and the topic out of the way, you're ready to move on to your actual point. Don't confuse your topic with your point. They aren't the same thing. My topic for this chapter is effective communication, but my point is that a communication formula will help you communicate effectively on a consistent basis. Figure out what you're trying to say and start with that. By doing this, you make it easier for your audience to listen to you, and they won't feel you're taking their valuable time.

The idea of coming right out and stating the point of a message feels unnatural to a lot of us because in school we're conditioned to build up to a point. We are asked to write multi-page essays that go on and on and state a thesis only at the very end. This communication style is okay because the teacher wants it that way and is paid to read and mark our assignments. But it doesn't work in the real world, where people don't get paid to listen to us and give us a minimum amount of their time and attention.

Stating your point quickly and concisely is important

when it comes to all aspects of professional life, even something as simple as requesting a meeting with someone. Before you ask for that meeting, make sure you're clear on your point or objective. What do you want to get out of the meeting?

At a college lecture I was giving, a student raised a concern about my get-to-the-point strategy. He wanted to know what to do if you wanted to impress a group of people but didn't have a point prepared. "If you wait to think of a point, the conversation may pass you by," he said, "so isn't it better to just jump in and start speaking without thinking?"

I told him, and I would say this to anyone looking for communication advice: "If you're trying to impress someone and don't have a point to make, do not speak. In that situation, the best thing you can do is keep quiet and listen. You will never impress someone by speaking without thinking of a clear point first."

Although "The Point" is the most important part of the message, the bulk of your time should be spent explaining your point. I call this "The Breakdown." I like to break down my point by using and presenting a list of categories – and the fewer categories, the better. Doing this makes it easier for presenters to organize their thoughts and for audiences to absorb a large amount of information. This is especially important when it comes to complicated topics because it reassures the audience that the matter will be explained in a simple manner.

Now you're ready for your recap and conclusion. Many people talk about the importance of finishing strong, but starting strong is more important. Why? Because you can't guarantee that your audience will stick around for the finish. Besides, if you have a strong start, your conclusion will naturally be strong because it's basically a recap of how you started. I like to finish my message not only by restating my point but also by encouraging action from my audience.

The following is an example of the message formula we have been discussing.

WELCOME: My name is Danny Pehar, and public speaking is a big part of my life.

TOPIC: My topic for today is Effective Communication.

THE POINT: By following a communication formula, you can be good at effective communication all the time.

THE BREAKDOWN: I plan to break my communication formula into four categories: The Welcome, The Topic, The Point and The Breakdown.

CATEGORY 1 - The Welcome: During an intro you must say your name and your relevance to the topic at hand.

CATEGORY 2 - The Topic: Clearly stating your topic will help clarify things for you and your audience.

CATEGORY 3 - The Point: The Point is the most important part of your message. Why are you speaking? What's your point?

CATEGORY 4 - The Breakdown: Your Breakdown lets the audience know how you will present your point.

RECAP: Therefore, when you follow the communication formula I describe here, you can be good at effective communication all the time, even when coming from a position of weakness.

ACTION: I encourage you to practice using this formula whether you're answering a question, delivering a presentation, running a meeting or just speaking with friends.

By following this formula, you can be a good communicator, but if you want to be a great communicator, I would encourage you to add three more pieces to your messaging tool kit: flow (the order in which you deliver your message), stories and self-promotion.

Many times, how a message flows is the difference between whether it comes alive or falls flat. Let me give you an example using the numbers below:

9 27 51 4101153811241631

If I asked you to memorize these numbers and then five seconds later asked you what they were, you'd probably find it difficult. Even if you're great with numbers, you'd probably forget in enough time. However, what if I rearranged the numbers into an easier pattern like this?

1 2 3 4 5 6 7 8 9 10 11 12 13 14 15

The numbers are easier to memorize now because they're in a pattern our brain easily recognizes. The numbers are exactly the same in both examples; the only difference is their order.

Throughout my career I've been asked to rework various people's messages, whether for a marketing campaign or a sales initiative. Often I don't change any of their content by adding or deleting information; I simply rework the *order* of their content. The new message is always extremely well received, even though all I did was rearrange the words. As in the numbers example, the right order can make all the difference.

To determine the perfect order, I once again follow a simple formula. I ask myself three questions:

1. Why does this matter to my audience?

2. Why does this matter to me?

3. How does what I'm saying relate to my next point?

Remember, there is no such thing as too much flow. I've never heard someone say, "That message flowed too well" or "That message was too easy to listen to." True message masters not only make one point segue into the next, they also make every word and every sentence flow smoothly into one another. As a result, their listeners find themselves in agreement with the message even before it's finished.

There's no reason why that message master can't be you. All you need to do is follow the formula described here.

Stories, the second extra to add to your messaging tool kit, will make your message pop. The great thing about stories is that many times you don't need to rework them. You just tell them naturally and exactly as they happened, and your audience will love them. The trick is to understand where to fit stories within your message.

One day while in Ottawa for a speaking engagement,

I grabbed a cab and was surprised by how clean it was. I said to the driver, "This is the cleanest cab I've ever seen."

"You must be from Toronto," he replied.

I laughed and asked, "How did you know?"

"People from Toronto are always commenting on how clean my cab is, and they also always comment on how little I honk my horn."

"I guess we do honk our horns a lot, and some of our cabs are pretty dirty."

"Maybe you'd honk less if you just cleaned up a bit."

I was so amused by this conversation I thought it would be the perfect welcome story for my presentation at the event I was attending. And all I had to do was put it in the right spot in my message and then tell it just as it had happened.

When I started my message, I welcomed the audience and thanked them for having me. Then I commented on how I was visiting from Toronto and thought their city was beautiful. From there, I went straight into my cab story. The audience loved it. After they were warmed up, I told them my topic and continued with my message.

The secret to the success of that story was its placement, and this is so for any story. For example, make sure you don't put a welcome-appropriate story in your topic section or your breakdown section.

I keep a document with a list of stories for my various types of communication. Anytime I hear a story I think might work in a presentation or project I'm working on, I add it to my list. For example, I would make note of my cab story with a brief description of how it could be used; in this case it would be labeled as a "Welcome Story." Whenever I'm building a message, I choose stories from my list and place them in the appropriate part of my effective communication formula.

You can add as many stories as you like to a message, as long as you honor your time commitments and stay on point. As important as stories are, they are there to help you get your point across. Don't lose yourself in a story. A solid understanding of your point will help keep you on track.

The third extra for your effective communication tool kit is self-promotion. Don't be afraid to promote yourself. People often downplay what they're going to do. At the beginning of their talk, they may something like, "I'm kinda sick. I have a cold, so this won't be my best" or "I didn't have a lot of time to prepare, so I apologize in advance." The theory behind this tactic is to under-promise and hopefully over-deliver. "If I tell everyone I'm a terrible speaker," the presenter may be thinking, "all I have to do is not pass out and they'll be impressed."

Here's the problem with that: the under-promise, over-deliver approach works only when you're talking about quantifiable facts – pure information like dates or financial matters. However, in a presentation where the audience's feelings and emotions come into play and can't be quantified, the mood you set helps determine the outcome. When you put yourself down before you start your message, you immediately downplay the mood for your audience and do yourself a huge disservice.

Think about the last time you were at a concert or a sporting event. What did the MC say before the event started? Did he apologize and tell the audience the event wasn't going to be that good because the team or rock star was tired? Or did he scream into the microphone,

"This is going to be greatest night of your life!"? MCs get audiences to where they need to be and make it easier on the entertainers.

When it comes to presentations or any sort of message, don't be afraid to be your own MC. Tell people you are going to be awesome and they will see you as awesome because you are awesome!

8

Being Awesome at Inspiring Others to Take Action

I remember watching the *X-Men* movies and thinking, "Wow, if someone was like Professor X and could control people's minds, that person could literally take over the world!"

Mind control might not be possible, but that doesn't mean we can't influence the minds of others to get what we want. When we have the power to influence, the world becomes an incredibly awesome place.

But *how* do we influence, inspire and persuade people to take action? This topic naturally flows from the previous chapter's focus on how to organize your thoughts so people can easily understand your message. Contrary to popular belief, when it comes to influence, you shouldn't approach this delicate art as a salesperson, because nobody likes to be sold to. Approach it as a teacher instead, because people like to be educated. Educate your audience, friends, family and business partners regarding why they should agree with your idea and explain how they can take action.

Like a teacher, you need to focus on the content as well as the student (the person you're trying to influence).

So let's start with the content, in other words, the offer or the idea. When you're trying to sell or inspire people to take action, you should indicate their Need for something. Then acknowledge the Challenge they may face in acquiring that need. Next, present your Offer, or your Idea, which addresses their need and takes into account the challenge. Finally, explain Why your Offer/Idea is the best option for them.

Let's say I want some of my friends to join me in buying an exercise video. I may say something like, "Guys, we all know we need to get in shape so we can look our best for our upcoming trip in three months, but we also know we don't have a lot of time to work out or a lot of money to spend on getting in shape. That's why I want to talk to you about this exercise video I came across that I think we should buy. The video is really inexpensive, and it'll help get us in shape by the time we leave for our trip just by exercising only a few minutes a day."

Let's recap the Need, Challenge, Offer and Why in the example above.

The NEED: "We all know we need to get in shape so we can look our best for our upcoming trip in three months."

The CHALLENGE: "We don't have a lot of time to work out or a lot of money to spend on getting in shape."

The OFFER/IDEA: "That's why I want to talk to you about this exercise video I came across that I think we should buy."

The WHY: "The video is really inexpensive, and it'll help get us in shape by the time we leave for our trip just by exercising only a few minutes a day."

If the need to get in shape combined with the challenge of time and money is in fact accurate, then acknowledging the need and challenge up front will convince your audience to listen with an open mind to what you have to say before you've even stated your offer/idea.

Understanding and stating the need and challenge behind any offer at the outset will make your success rate sky-rocket. In most cases, a properly executed explanation of your audience's need and challenge is when your audience decides whether they'll agree with you. The rest is just a matter of logistics – explaining your actual idea or your offer and then following that up with why your idea is the way to go, which basically ties right back to the need and the challenge you've already established.

In your why portion, you can list other brag points or quantifiable facts that support your offer. In the example of the workout video, you can list the higher prices of other videos or compare it with gym membership prices, or you can show stats on how much weight others have lost with the video you're pitching. Just remember to start with the need and the challenge. Too many people jump right in to their offer/idea without laying the proper groundwork first, which only gets the audience's defenses up. As I've mentioned, nobody likes to be sold to, but they do like to be educated.

Like any good teacher, you can't just focus on the content; you must also focus on the student. By focusing on the content, you may be able to convince your audience that your idea is great, but if you don't tell them what you need them to do, your attempt to inspire them to take action may fall flat. Remember, it's about more than just convincing people that your idea is great. It's about getting people to act on your idea. Once you've explained your idea (Content), you need to make it relevant to your specific audience (Student).

Let's go back to the exercise video example. I would go on, after listing the need, challenge, offer and why, to say, "Think about how good you're going to look on our vacation, and you'll still have so much spending money for the trip because the video is so inexpensive. You need to order this video tonight so you get it in time. All you need to do is go online and order from the company's website and the video will be delivered in three days. I'll send you the link by email right now. Let me know if you have any questions."

This example contains three important elements that will help ensure your audience acts on your idea.

First, appeal to your audience's personality by explaining why they specifically would like your idea. I call this the Personalized Why.

Next, explain the Action, or What you need them to complete. To have a higher chance of success, connect your action to a time line. (Remember to follow up with the person you're dealing with by setting a reminder in your calendar, as explained in chapter 6.)

Lastly, you give an Instruction, or How your client/friend/colleague can complete the action.

Let's recap these as used in the example:

THE PERSONALIZED WHY: "Think about how good you're going to look on our vacation, and you'll still have so much spending money for the trip because the video is so inexpensive."

THE ACTION/THE WHAT: "You need to order this video tonight so you get it in time."

THE INSTRUCTION/THE HOW: "All you need to do is go online and order from the company's website and the video will be delivered in three days. I'll send you the link by email right now."

The difference between the personalized why in the student section and the why from the content section is the subject of focus. In the content section the subject of focus is the offer/idea and why my offer/idea is great. In the student section, it is the audience. Why *you* want my offer/idea.

What I love best about this formula is how well it plugs in to the message formula explained in the previous chapter. I've used this formula successfully many times, whether I'm in a boardroom and selling a multimillion-dollar contract or with family and friends selling an idea like buying an exercise video.

The following is a quick cheat sheet.

The Content

THE NEED: What is the need for your idea?

THE CHALLENGE: What is the challenge of meeting the need that your idea addresses?

THE OFFER/IDEA: What is your offer or idea that addresses both the need and challenge you've just described?

THE WHY: Why is your offer/idea better than other offers/ideas?

The Student

THE PERSONALIZED WHY: Why should your audience be interested in your idea? What does it do for them specifically?

THE ACTION/THE WHAT: What does your audience need to do next? What is the simple action that needs to be taken and what is the time line?

THE INSTRUCTION/THE HOW: How should your audience act on your idea?

Based on the formula above, you can see that by understanding the needs of your audience and the challenges they may be facing, you can deliver a far more influential message.

Furthermore, understanding what drives your audience will give you a much more effective personalized why, which will further increase your success rate. Knowing this information is key. If your material is aimed at the benefits of losing weight, and your audience doesn't care about weight loss, then you're wasting your time by focusing on a need and challenge that won't capture them.

To influence any audience, you must find out what makes them tick, what inspires them and what motivates them. Start by asking questions like:

What keeps you up at night?

If you could fix anything about your life (or company), what would it be?

In an ideal world, what would be the perfect solution to fix the problem you just described?

What are your plans and goals for the next five years?

What are your biggest challenges?

If you could ask a genie for three wishes, what would they be?

Who are your heroes and why?

Questions like these will help reveal the drivers of your audience and will help you understand how they think and what they want. This information will enable you to plug your idea in to their desires.

I have a friend who is extremely talented at web design. What she can do with a web page is a thing of art and beauty. This same friend, however, is not a big student of what I covered in chapter 6. She doesn't follow basic time commitments. Unfortunately for her, many of her clients need things done on a strict schedule, so she's lost a lot of business to less-skilled competitors.

I tell this story not to reiterate the importance of following the basics but to demonstrate that, if you don't give the person you're trying to influence or impress what they want, it doesn't matter what else you give them. If meeting time commitments is the most important thing to a client or prospective employer, showing off your design skills in a presentation won't influence them if you don't honor that time commitment. If quality of work is most important, your low prices won't influence them.

In other words, the secret to getting what you want is knowing what they want.

Find out the needs of your audience, their personal goals and desires and the challenges they face in reaching those goals. Then plug that information in to the formula from this chapter, and you'll be able to influence anyone to do just about anything.

9

An Awesome Résumé for an Awesome Job Interview

I was excited about enrolling in college because I was taking Radio and Television Broadcasting. But I was nervous about telling my parents. They were simple, hard-working immigrants. I figured they would think broadcasting was an industry where no one could find a real job. But they were happy for me. They kept telling all their friends how much money I was going to make. This was such a pleasant surprise, because the radio and television industry wasn't known for the money it paid. They seemed to have more confidence than I did.

One night after I was well into the program, we had some guests over. We were all sitting around watching TV when suddenly it went all staticky.

My dad looked at me proudly and said, "Son, why don't you show us what you can do?"

A bit confused, I asked, "What are you talking about, Dad?"

"Show us what you can do with the TV."

"What am I supposed to do with the TV?"

"Stop joking around and show us what you learned in school and fix the TV."

Hmmm...perhaps my parents' confidence in the broadcasting world was not what I thought it was.

So I said, "Dad, why would I know how to fix a TV? I have no idea how to fix a TV."

Everybody in the room went quiet.

"What do you mean you have no idea how to fix the TV?" he said. "You've been going to school for radio and TV for almost two years now. You're getting good grades. Why can't you fix the TV?"

"This is going to be unpleasant," I thought.

"Dad, I'm not going to school to learn how to fix radios and televisions. I'm taking Radio and Television Broadcasting so I can be the guy *in* the TV."

My dad was utterly shocked. "But you can make so much money fixing TVs. Everyone has a TV, and they always break."

"But Dad, that's not what I want to do." I looked to my mother for some help in this argument, but she looked up at the ceiling, made the sign of the cross and said, "Please, God, help my son."

Before I could respond, my dad said, "You mean to tell me I have been paying for your college all this time thinking you're going to be fixing TVs, meanwhile, you're planning on dancing in the TV?"

"Dad, why would I be dancing? Who said anything about dancing? And you're not paying for my school – I am."

"Where do you live?"

"Here."

"Do I charge you rent?"

"No."

"Do I charge you to eat?"

"No."

"Do I charge you anything?"

"No."

"Well then, I'm paying for your college."

That was a rough night for my parents. In their minds, I went from becoming a rich television repairman to becoming a poor, unemployed dancing man on television. In fairness to them, they had a very tough life, and their main concern was whether I would be able to find gainful employment and support myself.

I still get calls to this day from friends of my parents asking me to fix their TVs.

All of my parents' concerns went away when I got my first full-time job working at a radio station. As long as I was making full-time money, they didn't care what I had studied in school.

As many fears as my parents had, I have to admit leaving school was really scary for me as well. Looking for work can be tough and demoralizing whether you're a student or an experienced professional. I soon learned a good résumé can be your best friend whether you're looking for new employment or you're up for a promotion.

In fact, when it comes to using communication to influence or persuade someone, not many things are going to be as important to you as your résumé and your job interview skills. Even if you love your job and the organization you work for, it's always a good idea to have a résumé on hand. In the event that you're promoted, your employer may want to have a current one on file for your new position. Of course, an awesome résumé is especially important for recent graduates entering the workforce for the first time.

A good résumé may not get you the job, but it will get you an interview. That's why it doesn't need to list everything you've ever done. Instead, it should serve as a good snapshot of why someone should take the time to meet with you.

In the past, other than their name and address, most people started their résumé with an objective, indicating they were looking for some sort of gainful employment. In today's advanced world, that is no longer necessary because a résumé itself indicates you want a job. Instead, use this prime real estate to create a Professional Profile for yourself – three or four sentences that explain why you're awesome.

Next, create a highlights section. Most people put brag points under each job on their list. Your résumé will pop much more if you group all your major brag points and put them in the same section. Anything that is a quantifiable fact is best, for example: "I saved my company 50%..." or "I increased efficiency by 25%..." If you've ever saved money or time or increased profits or efficiency, quantify it and put it in your highlights section. Another example of a quantifiable fact is years of experience you have in a particular industry or number of times you won a particular award for your field of expertise. Title this summary Career Highlights. If you haven't had a career but a series of jobs, simply title it Highlights.

Now you're ready for your Career History section. If

you haven't had a career, put down Employment History instead. Keep things short because you've already done all your bragging in the Highlights section. Instead, use this part of your résumé to tell potential employers where you've worked and how long you worked there. Add only a few words on what your responsibilities were at each job.

By separating Career Highlights from Career History, you make it easy for anyone looking at your résumé to find out why you're awesome. Ideally, you want to tell an awesome story about yourself in as little space as possible, preferably one page.

Your education and certification always come last because employers prefer knowing about proven results through experience.

Make sure you check with all of your contacts before you use them as references and try to find out beforehand what they plan to say about you. I can't tell you how many times people have used references who did not give good feedback on their behalf.

For help in creating your next résumé, check my résumé template at www.AwesomeAtBeingAwesome.com.

In addition to your résumé, you're going to need a cover letter. Cover letters used to be very painful to write, requiring all kinds of formalities. Luckily, today they're much easier. Nowadays, a cover letter is an email that basically indicates your interest in the position you're applying for and points a potential employer's attention to your résumé.

Remember, the goal of the résumé is not to get you the job but to get you an interview. That being said, the goal of the cover letter is only to get an employer to open up the attached résumé. So don't oversell it.

The first step is getting them to actually open the email, so the subject line is very important. You want it to be the title of the position you're interested in. If you know the job reference number, add it to the subject line as well. Then write just enough in the body of the email to make them want to open the attachment and let your résumé do the work. Three short paragraphs will do.

In the first paragraph, introduce yourself and say something flattering about the company or position you're applying for. For example:

I would like to take my career to the next level by joining Company ABC, the world's leader in awesomeness. (Check their website to see how they refer to themselves and use it here in the cover letter.)

In your second paragraph, include just a few sentences that sum you up nicely. If you can, add a quantifiable fact about yourself from the Career Highlights section of your résumé, something that shows how you've saved a company time or money, or how you made it money. You can also comment on your years of experience.

With over 10 years of widget experience, I am currently a widget maker at Company XYZ. In addition to creating compelling and all around awesome widgets, I have produced thingamabobs, doohickeys and other awesome things, saving my company 20% in production costs year after year. I am also a key contributor of ideas to our management team.

Now you're ready, in your third paragraph, to finish your cover letter. Indicate your interest in meeting and point them to your résumé. For example:

I hope to bring my skills and experience to Company ABC, and I look forward to meeting with you to discuss my attached résumé and any possible opportunities.

Take a careful look at the job posting and try to use its wording in your letter. If the employer is looking for a hard-working person, make sure you add "hard-working person" in your second paragraph, the one that describes you. The more you use their terminology, the better connection you'll forge. If there is no job position and you're just sending a blind résumé, use descriptive words from their website. For samples of how to reply to a job posting, check out www.AwesomeAtBeingAwesome.com.

Once you get past the cover letter and résumé stage, it's time for the job interview. Remember that the main question behind the interview is, "Why should I hire you?" The question may not actually be asked, but make no mistake, it's what you're there to answer. Try to weave it in to every answer you give. Don't lose focus by getting lost answering anything else.

For example, I like doing stand-up comedy, and I was asked about it in a job interview earlier in my career. I love talking about comedy. I could have gone on and on about my material, what it's based on and how I prepare for a show. But instead I brought the focus right back to why I should be hired. I replied, "Having the focus to prepare for a comedy show has made me a better employee." Then I gave an example to back it up.

The lesson here is not unlike the main lesson of chapter 7. What is the point of your presentation? At a job interview your point is that you're the right person for the job.

Also, it's a good idea before any job interview to review and even rehearse your story. That way, when an interviewer asks you to tell them about yourself, you can tell a quick but informative story about your experience, your work ethic and your strategies; why previous employers liked you; and why you're looking for a new job. You also want to be ready with job-related accomplishments. Quickly pulling from stories you have in your head will make your responses that much more impressive.

You also want to be prepared for common questions like, "What is your goal for the next five years?" or "What are your greatest strengths?" Your answers will be awesome as long as you remember to pull from your ready-made material and make sure every answer ties back to the only question that truly matters: "Why should I hire you?"

If you get hit with the dreaded "What is your greatest weakness?" question, avoid the typical answer of "I work too hard." Most interviewers have stopped asking this question, but those who still do have gotten too smart for that typical answer. They recognize you're only disguising a strength as a weakness. Instead, reveal a real weakness that isn't relevant to the job and won't hurt your chances of getting hired.

I was interviewed for a job once that involved a lot of public speaking. When asked about my weakness, I said it was filling out expense reports. I did this because

I knew they were an insignificant part of the job I was applying for. I even made a joke about how bad I was at them. My interviewer talked about his own frustrations with these reports, and we both had a laugh. Then I turned it around and said, "I prefer to be actually working rather than spending time filling out reports."

Also, during the interview, don't be afraid to show that you really want the job. Remember the story from chapter 5 about the enthusiastic candidate I hired who said he wanted the job so badly he'd even sweep floors? It's important to show interest. The interview is not the place to play it cool and pretend you're not interested. Show your excitement and appreciation. You can do this by spending some time looking at the company's website before your interview. Your research will help you prepare some relevant questions for your interviewer and show you're eager to get the job.

As mentioned in the previous chapter, the best way to get what you want from someone is to know what they want. Researching the company will help you understand their goals and vision. If the prospective company prides itself on providing quality work to its customers, paint a picture of how important quality is to you. Give some examples of ways you have proven this in the past. If the company prides itself on speed, give examples of how you've helped other organizations run faster.

Also, when studying the company you're interviewing with, be sure to notice the terminology they use. For example, if they refer to their clients as "members" or as "family," make sure you use that same language. If you plan to tell a story that demonstrates how you can help an organization maximize quality for its clients, and you noticed in your research that they call their clients members, say something like, "I can help you provide quality service to your members." If they're big on using the term "family," say something like, "I will take great pride in serving family."

This may feel a little weird sometimes, but by speaking the same language as the company you want to work for, you show two things: first, that you came to the interview prepared, which is the kind of employee you are; and second, that you "get it."

When an organization makes a hire, they're taking a chance. They don't want to hire someone who won't fit their corporate culture. The best way to show that you fit the culture of any organization is to speak their language. The best way to do this is to study them. Go to the About page on their website and read their mission statement. This will usually give you a firm understanding of their goals, what's important to them and, of course, how they speak about these important things.

When it's time for the question portion of the interview, don't be afraid to ask your interviewer questions like, "How long have you worked here?" and "What's your favorite part of the company?" This will show you're interested not only in the business but also in the person interviewing you. People love to talk about themselves. Get your interviewer talking about their accomplishments and make them feel good.

I remember this one job I really wanted. I was being escorted to the interview room by the interviewer and it turned out to be quite a long walk, so I made small talk and asked him how long he had worked at the company and what he liked most about his job. The interviewer went on to tell me about a big project he had completed that he was proud of. The story continued once we were in the room, and the interviewer got more and more passionate about it.

Towards the end of that story, the interviewer started asking me a few questions and then said, "Well, Danny, I really enjoyed talking to you. I'd like to offer you the job."

I got the job on the spot, but I spoke only 5% of the time. As I've mentioned, people want to hire and work with people they like. Be one of those people by showing interest, and your chances of getting the job and career you want will sky-rocket.

It's also important to note that the interview isn't over when it's over. One of the most important things you can do is to follow it up with a thank you. I learned that in connection with the job interview for my first office job. It was for an entry-level position pretty much anyone could do. I sensed the interviewer just wasn't into the interview. He looked bored. My guess is he felt the interviews were a waste of his time. He was so bored, I couldn't get a read on him. I had no idea whether I stood a chance of getting the job. While he might not have cared who got hired, I felt working for that company would be perfect for me.

The next day, I was talking to a friend and telling him about the interview. I told him I really wanted the job but had no idea how the interviewer felt about me. My friend gave me amazing advice. "If you really want the job," he said, "call the interviewer and thank him for his time. Don't ask him any questions about your chances, just thank him for his time."

That's exactly what I did. Five minutes later, the

interviewer called me back and in a very bored voice said, "Danny, I got your voicemail and, umm, if you want the job, it's yours."

My guess is I didn't really impress him during the interview but neither did anyone else. However, I'm fairly sure I was the only prospect who called to thank him. And that little thank you is what started me off on an amazing career!

When your interview is over, whether you feel your chances are strong or slim, thank your interviewer for their time and ask for a business card, as well as when they think they'll be making their decision. Later that same day, send your interviewer an email and thank them again for their time. Again, don't ask any questions about the job. Just tell them you're excited about the potential of working for their company and you're grateful for the pleasant interview. When all things are equal between you and the other applicants, something as simple as a polite follow-up may be all it takes to tip things in your favor.

There's another thing I really want to stress, especially for younger readers. When you're looking for a job, don't get your mother to make the call. And parents, do yourself and your kids a favor by having them make their own calls. I have a lot of friends who work in HR. They say a growing issue is parents calling companies to set up interviews for their children. I'm not referring to parents who happen to have a contact at an organization and are putting in a good word for their offspring. I'm talking about helicopter parents who are looking at public job posts and applying to jobs on behalf of their children.

The best way for you to look at it is this: if you're too immature to set up your own interview and you need your mom to do it, you're too immature for the job. If your mom is calling me for a job, I know you don't want it.

Kids, if you want the job, set up your own interview.

Parents, if you want your kids to get the job, make sure they make the call.

I also want to address salary negotiation, but I want to be very careful with this topic. If you're a young person just out of school, aggressive salary negotiation isn't a good idea. When you're looking for that first job and don't have a lot of experience, don't be too picky. Don't take anything you hate, but if it's in your field of study, try to be open-minded. We all have to start somewhere. I don't think there's ever been a time when the job market for new graduates has been good. If you're too picky, you'll lose out. That low-salary first job could be your entry point to many opportunities.

I've made a beautiful career for myself by taking opportunities no one else wanted. As I explained in chapter 5, it's important to look past a problem and see the opportunity. Once you get the job, focus on having the right attitude, excelling at the basics and communicating effectively. The money will follow.

When I first got in to sales, my friends poked fun at me and asked, "Have you made any money today?"

I always said, "Right now, it's not about the money. Right now, it's about learning to be good."

Focus on being good, and the money will come.

It's quite a different story for those of you who have been around a while and have proven experience in a particular field and aren't just good but awesome.

Negotiation can help you get the money you deserve. The trick is to avoid overthinking it. Some people suggest researching the going rate for your industry and desired job and using that as leverage to get your desired amount. That strategy has some merit to it. However, I find the negotiation process much easier when I do some soul-searching to determine what I need the salary to be for me to take the job. Once I know this number, I know I'm not going to take anything less.

Assuming the number is realistic and you're prepared to walk if you don't get it, one of two things is going to happen. You'll either get the job at the number you want or you won't get the job, which is fine because it's under the number you want. Nail the interview and make them love you, then figure out what your number needs to be. The rest is easy.

The pathway to having an awesome career is finding an awesome job, and the pathway to an awesome job is an awesome cover letter, résumé and interview. An awesome cover letter will get a future employer to look at your résumé, an awesome résumé will get you an interview and an awesome interview will get you the job. When you're dealing with a potential new employer or a promotion, remember that the main questions you're there to answer are ones that may never be openly asked: Why should I hire you? What makes you awesome? Be sure to think about this clearly and build it in to your cover letter, résumé and interview.

You're already awesome. Now you just need to make sure your future employer knows it.

10

Spending the Rest of Your Life with the Perfect Partner

*I*N chapters 5, 6 and 7, I explored the importance of having a good attitude, following the basics and learning to communicate effectively in order to build good relationships at work and at home. Perhaps the most important relationship is the one we have with our significant other.

For me, it was a girl named Patricia who caught my eye. We met in high school, and it didn't take long before I was in love. My parents hated Patricia, though, and not for any legitimate reason. They just didn't like that her ethnicity was different from ours.

I remember my dad saying, "She's only using you."

I'd be like, "Using me for what? I've got no money, I work at Chuck E. Cheese's and I don't have a car."

My dad would say, "She's using you because you're good!"

I'm sure that's what she was doing, using me for my goodness. Because that's what bad girls do, right? They go out and find a boy with no financial assets and use them for their goodness.

It wasn't entirely my dad's fault, though. He was a simple man. He didn't like change, so he didn't want his only son to marry outside of what he knew. To give you an idea of how much this man doesn't like change, let me put it this way: My dad has been living in Canada for 45 years and in that time he has managed to visit only a grocery store, a church and his work. That's about the extent of what he knows about Canada, and that's all he wants to know.

Eventually my parents got over the fact I was dating someone of a different nationality and learned to appreciate Patricia as a person, so I was able to enjoy my girlfriend in peace.

One day, Patty and I were walking in a mall, and we were both hungry, so we decided to go to Burger King. Patty said she was going to go grab us a table and asked me to get her a Whopper.

No problem, right? But as I was standing in line, I realized she never gave me any money. I guess when she asked me to get her a Whopper, she meant get her a Whopper and then pay for it. Wow, this was new to me. Going to school with white skates as a boy meant I didn't have a lot of girlfriends. Okay, until now, not one. Suddenly my expenses were doubling. Oh well, nobody said having a girlfriend was going to be cheap.

So I ordered two Whoppers, one of the two with bacon. I loved bacon with my Whopper. It was 50 cents extra, but I splurged for the good stuff. I figured Patty wouldn't mind not getting it on hers. After all, she was getting an entire Whopper for free.

But two seconds after I sat down, she said, "Hey, you've got bacon on your Whopper. Why didn't you get any on mine?"

"Oh, uh, yeah," I said nervously. "I guess I must have forgotten. Sorry."

Then she said, "That's okay, I'll just take some out of yours and put it in mine."

Ummm, wow! So now I have to pay for an extra Whopper and on top of that give away bacon I got just for me? I worked hard to pay for that bacon, and as a guy who was new to dating, I wasn't used to sharing. It was fun having a girlfriend, but was it worth a Whopper with bacon?

Yes, of course it was. A good relationship, like anything in life, takes some work, compromise and even sacrifice, even if the sacrifice is sharing your bacon.

I ended up marrying that girl. We had a great wedding day, but we've had an even greater marriage. I feel like I live with my buddy combined with someone I just started dating, because being with her still feels new and exciting. We go out on date nights every week and laugh and goof off so often that we pretty much have our own language. And we buy each other bacon Whoppers all the time.

Every now and then a family member or friend asks me why my marriage is so successful. I always say it started with picking the right partner.

When I was younger, my parents always told me it was important to marry a girl with the same religious and cultural background and that she should come from a good family. The fact that Patty's family was Portuguese was a real problem for them.

Many of us have been given similar pieces of advice, and, yes, although the advice has some merit, I've seen a lot of marriages fail even when both people come from good families and the same religion and culture. As a matter of fact, having predefined expectations like this can get in the way of finding the right person.

I believe the best way to pick the right partner is actually much simpler than culture or religion. All you really need to consider is this: Do you enjoy spending time with each other without needing other people around or without even doing anything special? If the answer is yes, that's a great start. When everything else gets old, the desire to spend time with that person won't.

If you ask the average adult how many boyfriends or how many girlfriends they've had, you'll hear a wide range of numbers. But if you ask how many best friends they've had, the answer is usually much smaller. Boyfriends and girlfriends come and go, but best friends are few and far between. Marry your best friend and your partnership will not only survive, it will blossom into genuine happiness regardless of your cultures, religious beliefs or family backgrounds.

Some of you may be thinking, "I've been married for years now. Picking the right partner can't help me because I chose one a long time ago and can't remember why I thought they were right." Whether you've picked the right partner or feel you could have chosen better, a good marriage takes work. Take time for each other. Many times in life, things get out of hand. As I mentioned in chapter 2, we lose balance when we focus too much on one aspect of life and neglect another. We can't neglect our relationship and expect it to take care of itself.

Here are a few simple tips to help you respect and appreciate each other:

1. **Compliment each other often**. It's the easiest way to make someone's day.

2. **Hug each other daily**. It's so simple, but so powerful. And it's a fun way to stay happy and close.

3. **Put down your mobile device!** This tip is applicable to any relationship. When talking to someone, interact with THEM, not your mobile device. Old-fashioned common courtesy makes a world of difference to any relationship.

4. **Say please and thank you**. They're called the magic words for a reason. When you want something, be nice and say please. When you get something, show your appreciation and say thank you. You'll be amazed how this very simple tip can change your life – in all of your relationships.

5. **Be accountable**. Do what you say you're going to do when you say you're going to do it or give a reason why it can't be done. I'm borrowing this advice from chapter 6 because it's very applicable here. Nobody likes to feel they can't rely on their partner. Follow this tip and you'll greatly reduce your arguments.

6. **Have a regular date night**. Make time for it no matter how busy you are and remind each other why you wanted to be together in the first place.

By following these tips, you and your partner will argue a lot less, but you will still argue. Even the most loving couples fight. Being married is wonderful, but like anything in life, some days are harder than others, and that's okay.

One day I was in the bathroom wiping my hands and Patty walked in and started freaking out.

"What are you doing?" she asked.

"What's it look like I'm doing? I'm wiping my hands."

"Those are the show towels, you idiot."

"Show towels? What on earth is a show towel?"

"These towels aren't meant to be used. They're just meant to hang on the wall and look nice, you know, for show."

Now I don't know much about home décor, but most people I know like to hang paintings or pictures. My wife hangs towels.

A lot of the fights between Patricia and me result from our very different upbringings. I come from humble origins, and it doesn't take much to impress me. Patricia, on the other hand, comes from a world of show towels, and lowered toilet seats, for that matter, and isn't so easily impressed. But as much as we fight, we haven't killed each other yet – or even come close – and we always easily bounce back.

Some couples fight over a recurring issue. I know a couple who argue every time they go to a party. He always wants to stay late, and she wants to go home early. It starts out as a small, playful disagreement but turns ugly by the end of the night.

The good news here is that, when it comes to recurring issues, a little planning can help a lot.

Analyze your disagreements to see if there's a pattern. Maybe going to a certain place or hanging out with certain people brings out the worst in each of you. Once you recognize a pattern, wait until you're both calm and getting along. Sit down together and plan how you can avoid the same argument in the future.

For example, if it's something like the party example I described, consider arriving and leaving separately. That may sound like a bit of a hassle, but in the grand scheme of things, it's quite a small inconvenience if it prevents another major argument. If the party issue is really serious, consider avoiding them altogether until you can figure out how to both attend without fighting.

Many couples I've helped tell me it's not a question of having multiple fights over multiple issues but having multiple fights over the same issues. Find out what those issues are. Analyze your top five recurring fights. Sit down and talk about how you can avoid those minefields. With some simple planning, you can prevent a major disagreement and find a way to enjoy spending time together.

You'll still disagree, but that's normal. With the exception of abusive situations, fighting is okay. It means we're human. The trick is to not let the fights get out of hand.

Fights sometimes escalate because other issues are brought up. Older fights resurface and make their way into the current fight. Also, because you and your partner know each other really well, you know each other's weak points (e.g., one of you is insecure about body weight). All too often, those weaknesses are targeted (e.g., one partner insults the other about their weight).

Here are a few tips to prevent fights from getting out of hand:

1. **Have one fight at time**. When you have a disagreement and another topic is brought up from a previous fight, agree that you'll have only one fight at a time and put that topic aside. This is a very simple trick to keep arguments from escalating.

2. **Come up with the rules of war**. When you're both calm, list the words, insults or topics that are off limits in a fight. Sometimes all it takes is one insult to turn an argument into something ugly. The flip side is that avoiding insults can reduce a fight to a disagreement and eventually even to a compromise.

3. **Lower your voice**. Raising your voice actually gets your adrenaline pumping, which will make you even angrier. In addition, it forces your partner to try to match you. They raise their voice and *their* adrenaline starts pumping, making them even angrier. Before you know it, the rules of war go out the window, insults make their way into the fight and older fights are rehashed. Suddenly, an argument about washing the dishes becomes World War Three. Lower your voice and it will lower your anger, and likely your partner's anger also.

4. **Try to see it from the other's point of view**.
   Sometimes we get so angry at our partner, we
   don't even attempt to see why they did what they
   did. Just taking a few minutes to think about it
   and breathe will help you approach your partner
   without yelling, spewing insults or bringing up
   the past.

Now, if you're in the unfortunate situation where
your partner has abused you or cheated on you, my heart
goes out to you. I encourage you to get help, whether
from someone in your family or a professional. If you're
living in fear, whether fear of abuse or of being cheated
on, then something is wrong. You deserve to be treated
better!

Those of us not living in such severe circumstances
should remember that the pathway to a great marriage
starts with picking the right partner. Marry your best
friend and you'll be way more likely to find happiness.
Whether you've married your best friend or not, learn to
respect and appreciate each other and avoid recurring
issues. You'll fight less. When you do fight, the tactics
described here will help keep your fights from escalating. Follow these tips and your home life will reach
levels of happiness you never thought possible.

11

How to Save for Anything

*F*URTHER to the previous chapter on relationships, a common argument for couples revolves around finances. Whether you're single or in a relationship, understanding how to save is very important to your happiness.

Money isn't everything, but it sure makes some things much easier. I remember the day I realized my family was poor. It was incredibly unpleasant.

My sister and I used to play with pencil crayons, pretending they were dolls and action figures, and it was during one of those games that she broke the news to me.

"You know we're poor, right?" she said. "That's why all of our stuff sucks! Normal kids play with real dolls and action figures, not pencil crayons."

I was dumbstruck. Trying to deny her revelation, I said, "Hey, if we're so poor then why do we have such a big TV? Dad says it's 60 inches big."

Mind you, only 10 inches of it was actual screen; the rest was made out of wood, and when you turned the knobs it sounded like thunder. We actually got in trouble for changing the channels too fast because it made too much noise. "Don't change the channels so fast, your father's sleeping," my mother would say. Who has to worry these days about waking their parents because they're changing the channels too fast?

Anyway, I figured there was no way we could be poor. All of the houses on our street looked like ours did – no way could everyone on our street be poor! That's exactly what I thought. Until we were invited to dinner by a family outside our neighborhood.

We pulled up to this nice big house, and, once we got inside, the kids asked us if we wanted to watch TV. When we saw their television, my sister whispered to me, "See? That's what a real 60-inch TV is supposed to look like. The 60 inches is supposed to be the screen not the wood around the TV. This TV doesn't even have any wood."

"Well, I admit the big screen looks pretty cool," I said, "but if it doesn't have any wood, how are you supposed to hit it when it stops working? You'd break this TV if you hit it."

Any good TV should be able to survive a nice swift kick to the side, I always thought. What I didn't know was that you didn't need to hit these TVs. These televisions didn't stop working just because they'd been on for 20 minutes.

When our hosts turned on their legitimate 60-inch TV, a cartoon was on. For the first time, I saw a robot man turn into a truck, and I started to freak out.

"Did that man just turn into a truck?!" I yelled. "How the heck did that man turn into a truck?!"

As a kid, there's something about seeing a man turn into a truck for the first time that changes you.

"What, you've never seen *Transformers* before?" one of the kids asked.

All I could say was, "Did you see that man turn into a truck?"

You see, *Transformers* was on channel 21, but we didn't get anything past channel 10 except for channel U. You may be thinking, what's channel U? Well, I can't answer that question because I have no idea. All I know is we had a big U on our television knob that came after channel 10, and it broadcast static 24/7.

Seeing *Transformers* was eye opening, but what I saw next was mind blowing. The cartoon went to a commercial break, and the first ad was for Hot Wheels. A boy put some water on his Hot Wheels car, and it changed color.

I started to lose it. My young heart wasn't up for all this excitement.

I couldn't understand why the other kids weren't impressed. "Guys, are you watching the same thing I'm watching?" I asked.

"Yeah," one of them said, "but this commercial has been on for so long. You've never seen this before?"

"Of course I've seen this commercial before, but that's a different toy they're showing!"

The kids were positive it wasn't a new toy at all. I looked to my sister, who explained to me that the Hot Wheels toy looked different because I was seeing the commercial on a color TV for the first time. Our TV was black and white, so when the commercial came on at home, the cars never really changed that much.

It all made sense now. My sister was right. There was

a whole other world outside the one I knew, a world of color-changing cars and *Transformers*. We were, without a doubt, poor.

Knowing you're poor sucks, but it also helps you understand certain things about your life a little bit better.

One day we were getting ready to walk to school, and my mother noticed it was raining really hard. We didn't have any raincoats, but she had an idea. You see, being poor meant you sometimes had to be resourceful, and no one was more resourceful than my mother. It was this resourcefulness, though, that I sometimes really hated.

"Here, put these on," she said, holding up some garbage bags. "They'll keep you dry."

"We can't wear those," I said. "Those are garbage bags."

"Well, they'll keep you dry."

So there we were on our way to school surrounded by cute kids in their brightly colored raincoats while we wore black Glad garbage bags. I don't know for sure, but I'm fairly certain the person who came up with the name "Glad" never had to wear those things as a raincoat.

The great thing about growing up poor is there's no shortage of good stories. Then again, while being poor is great for character development, from a practical point of view, it has its obvious disadvantages. And as much as I appreciate a good story, I also appreciate having some money in my pocket and not having to wear a garbage bag when I leave the house.

Looked at from a basic perspective, there are only two elements to money: the money we make and the money we save. If you ask any financial expert, they'll tell you that the money we save is just as important as the money we make.

We've all heard the stories about famous people with millions who've gone broke. Or people who've won the lottery only to declare bankruptcy five years after their windfall. At first it almost seems impossible. How could someone with so much money go broke? But it's really quite simple. If you spend more than you make, eventually the money's going to run out.

Earlier I discussed career advancement and its importance to your mental fulfilment and financial success. But concentrating on your savings, in addition to making good financial sense, can also help you in your career.

I have a friend who makes terrible career choices because he's always up to his neck in debt. He makes his moves based not on long-term strategies that benefit his career but on short-term gains because he needs money and he needs it *now*.

When we used to work together, a bunch of his clients told him they were going to spend a lot of their budget with him in the next 12 months. He was going to have an amazing year; all he had to do was stay with the company. But he had made some bad financial choices and needed money quick, so he walked away from this amazing job and all of its opportunities to take a new job that was offering a signing bonus.

"Are you seriously walking away from all of this because of that small signing bonus?" I asked him.

He replied, "I have no choice. I need money now."

When your finances make you desperate, you'll be forced to make poor career choices. It will weaken your ability to negotiate for a job, not to mention the overall strain it will put on your life. As for my friend, he's always made good money. For the past 10 years, he's had a six-figure income and hasn't had any financial emergencies. He's just a terrible saver. He's always talking about all of the things he plans to buy once he gets his hands on some money.

After he took that new job, he got his signing bonus and told me he was going to purchase a guitar.

"Didn't you take that job because of your debt?" I asked. "Shouldn't you focus on that?"

He just shrugged and said, "I really want this guitar."

And therein lies his vicious cycle. He keeps spending without saving, his debts increase, then he starts making less money because of his poor career choices, which only worsens his debt.

With this in mind, I want to take some time to go over one of the easiest and most important plans I've ever made with regard to money.

As I was getting set to propose to my wife, I needed to save for an engagement ring, a mortgage down payment and a wedding. I was making good money at the time, but I hadn't been making much for a long time before that, so I only had $4K in the bank. I thought I was going to have a nervous breakdown...until I came up with a plan.

I call it DASG, Danny's Awesome Savings Goal (I'm not married to the name and am open to suggestions).

It's really simple.

First, consider how much money you make per month (for those of you whose pay changes depending on the month, take an average of what you've made over the last few months). Let's say the number is $3,000 a month, after taxes.

From there, make a list of what you know you're going to need to spend in a month – on bills, clothes or even just fun purchases.

After you've listed your expenses, subtract them from your total monthly earnings. The number you're left with is your monthly DASG. Let's say it's $1,000. If you know you can save that much a month, you know you have the ability to save $10,000 in 10 months. Now compare that amount with what you need to save for your long-range goals. For example, saving for a down payment on a house. If after making these calculations you see that $10,000 isn't enough for your 10-month savings goal, then you know very early on that you need to make changes. You can decide on paper the expenses you need to reduce to beef up that $10,000.

An important objective here is to find out if the monthly DASG you are saving will be enough for your overall goal. It would be terrible to spend all that time saving, and then, when it's too late, realize you still don't have enough money.

Once you've figured out the appropriate monthly DASG for your overall goal, you can easily monitor your progress. If something goes wrong with your spending (e.g., an unforeseen car repair expense), you'll know early on whether you're on track to hit your 10-month goal, and you can make changes if necessary. A big part of success in saving money is to avoid as many surprises as possible. So track your savings goals, along with your earnings, your spending and your savings deadline, and be prepared to make changes if necessary.

Put your monthly DASG aside before you spend any money. That way you guarantee that you'll have it. In the example we're using, that means putting $1,000 in to a savings account as soon as you're paid your monthly $3,000.

Regardless of what your savings goals are, there are four questions you need to answer:

1. How much time do I have to save up my desired amount?

2. How much money do I need to save from now until my savings deadline?

3. How much money will I make from now until my savings deadline?

4. What are my expenses from now until my savings deadline?

In some ways this lesson is similar to the ones on calorie-tracking (chapter 3) or obligation-tracking (chapter 6). Tracking goals on paper will increase your chances of success because you can clearly see what needs to be done.

And always remember, the amount you save is just as important as the amount you earn.

12

How to Make Your Savings Last the Rest of Your Life

IT'S hard for most of us to imagine saving up enough for retirement. Some people's retirement plan is to win the lottery. At one time, that was certainly one of my plans as well. As scary as the thought of saving enough to live off the rest of our lives may be, with just a little bit of planning, it's actually very doable.

The trick is to make compound interest work for you. Compound interest is interest that builds on itself: interest is added to an initial amount and the new amount earns interest and so on.

The true power of compound interest can be illustrated through a mathematics exercise often used in elementary school. Let's say I was to offer you a deal: you can have $1 million now or receive a penny today, two pennies tomorrow, four pennies on the third day, and so on for 30 days. Most people would take the $1 million, but, believe it or not, that would be taking the smaller amount.

If you look at the chart below, showing one month's worth of pennies being doubled daily, you'll see what I mean. It starts off slow. If you start with a penny and double the amount every day, you would only have 64 cents by the 7th day, and only $163.84 by the 15th day. However, if you kept doubling the daily amount, you would soon begin to see the true benefit of compound interest because the amount on the 30th day would be $5,368,709, not to mention the cumulative amount of all 30 days, which would be $10,737,418.

Doubling a Penny for 30 days Versus One Million Dollars									
Day 1	$0.01	Day 8	$1.28	Day 15	$163.84	Day 22	$20,971.52	Day 29	$2,684,354.56
Day 2	$0.02	Day 9	$2.56	Day 16	$327.68	Day 23	$41,943.04	Day 30	$5,368,709.12
Day 3	$0.04	Day 10	$5.12	Day 17	$655.36	Day 24	$83,886.08	Cumulative amount of all 30 days: $10,737,418.23	
Day 4	$0.08	Day 11	$10.24	Day 18	$1,310.72	Day 25	$167,772.16		
Day 5	$0.16	Day 12	$20.48	Day 19	$2,621.44	Day 26	$335,544.32		
Day 6	$0.32	Day 13	$40.96	Day 20	$5,242.88	Day 27	$671,088.64		
Day 7	$0.64	Day 14	$81.92	Day 21	$10,485.76	Day 28	$1,342,177.28		

The penny story is hated by many financial experts because, as we all know, being in a situation where our money is doubled, let alone doubled every day for 30 days, is highly unlikely. But I like it for its simplicity and educational value, because it shows those of us not familiar with compound interest how well even a small amount of money can grow when compounded over a sufficient period of time.

Let me give you a more realistic example. If I put $5,000 in to an investment and get an assumed 8% return in 12 months, I would make $400. The beauty here is that, if I leave the money in the investment and get an additional 8% return in another 12 months, I'm now making 8% off the $5,400, not the original $5,000. And 8% of $5,400 is $432 – that's $32 more than the previous year. That is compound interest working for you.

Let's take a look at a savings example that doesn't involve compound interest. If, at the age of 20, I set aside $200 a year and hide it in a shoebox and add $200 every year, when I turn 65 and add my final $200, I will have collected $9,200 over that 46-year period. However, if, at the age of 20, I take that $200 and put it in to an investment that generates an assumed annual 8% rate of return, and I add an additional $200 dollars annually to that investment, my total over the same 46-year period would be $90,380. That's nearly 10 times the $9,200 I would have saved without the proper use of compound interest.

Now let's take a much bolder look at this same example. I'm 20 years old, but instead of saving $200 a year, I do everything in my power to save $200 a month, which I do by using the savings tips in the previous chapter. With the same assumed 8% annual rate of return, I will have $1,084,560 by age 65. In other words, given enough time, with proper investing, saving even a small amount can make you a millionaire.

Now, some of you may think 8% is not a realistic rate of return. The fact is, any number I put in this book could be irrelevant next year and certainly will not be an indicator of what the future will have in store. I use 8% simply for demonstration purposes. What I want you to take from this is the importance of investing versus simply saving your money. It is precisely because we have no way of knowing what the future has in store that we need to plan for it very carefully. As I mentioned previously, other than winning the lottery, a lot of people feel they can never save up enough to retire, and some use this as an excuse to not bother planning at all. But it's not about saving every dollar; it's about saving enough that, when properly invested, it grows into the amount you need.

The goal is to build your money through compound returns high enough that you can live off the percentage of the return itself. In other words, when you retire, your yearly returns become your salary. In the example of $1,084,560, an assumed 8% return will generate an annual amount of $86,764. So even if you lived well past 100, your money wouldn't run out because, instead of taking out that million dollars and spending it when you retire, you will keep it where it is and live off its annual percentage of return.

Inflation, of course, will decrease the value of your return over the years, and there is no guarantee of what percentage return your investments will achieve. But combatting these drawbacks is the fact that your expenses will be reduced by that age. For example, you're unlikely to be making mortgage payments and/ or paying for child-care bills by that age. Regardless of the specifics of inflation versus reduced bills, you will be in a much stronger position compared with those who haven't planned like this.

You may be thinking, "But I don't understand anything when it comes to investing. How can I do this?"

Don't worry. Many professionals at financial institutions, banks and credit unions would be happy to discuss a retirement plan with you. And you don't need a lot of money to work with a financial planner. If all you can put aside is a couple hundred bucks a year, start with that. Like compound interest on a penny, you'll be amazed by how it will grow.

The best financial advice I can give anyone is to establish a good relationship with a financial planning professional. They can help you figure out the best strategies for you and your situation, including:

- How much you need to put away to live comfortably after you stop working

- Paying down debt and other priorities versus retirement planning

- How to take advantage of employer benefits and pension plans

This last one is really near and dear to my heart. For years I worked for a company with a fantastic matching pension plan. I never took advantage of it, because I simply had no idea why I should and how to do it. There was so much free money available to me, and I walked away from it, until a financial planner explained it to me. In short, the right planner will help you define an appropriate goal and put you on a plan to achieve it.

Be sure to keep in mind what I mentioned earlier – that the sooner you start saving, the more time compound interest has to grow.

Let's say I'm 25 years old and put $4,000 in to an investment that generates an assumed 8% annual return, and I keep adding $4,000 annually. At age 36 I add $4,000 one final time and decide to stop adding my own money and just let the interest do all the work. By the time I'm 69, I'll have $1,039,195, with only $48,000 of that being my actual investment over a 12-year period. The rest is all growth.

Now let's say I don't start investing until I'm 37, at which time I put $4,000 in to an investment that generates an assumed 8% annual return. I do this every year, and at age 69, after I add $4,000 one final time, my grand total comes to $630,507 – considerably less than the previous example and costing me $132,000 of my own money invested over a 33-year period.

Why is that? How come I spent more of my own money in the second example, with the assumed rate of return being the same, and made less? Because in the previous example I started at a younger age and had more time for the compound interest to grow.

All the investment examples used in this chapter are based on certain assumptions for educational purposes only and are not meant to guarantee investment values or returns. Don't get hung up on the specific numbers in the examples but focus on the takeaways. In a nutshell, there are five main things to remember when it comes to your money:

1. **Invest in something**. You'll never be prepared to retire through simple savings without the benefit of compound interest.

2. **Don't wait, get started right now**. The sooner you start, the better compound interest will work for you.

3. **Talk to a professional**. Make it easy on yourself and take out the guesswork. Any bank,

credit union or reputable financial adviser can help you with this.

4. **Talk to your kids about saving and investing wisely and get them started early**. You'll be doing yourself and them a huge favor. Too many people avoid talking to their kids about money.

5. **Be aware that compound interest can also be dangerous**. Imagine the penny story in reverse. If you OWE money, compound interest on your loan can eventually grow to a point where it gets completely out of your control. This kind of debt has ruined many lives. Be aware of your loans and incorporate a payment plan as learned in chapter 11 to make sure your debt doesn't get out of hand. Make compound interest work for you, not against you, and you will have a lot less stress in your life.

13

Bringing It All Together and Cutting Out What You Don't Need

*U*P to this point, I've given you numerous tips for succeeding in various aspects of life. But the true magic happens when you tie everything together and get your body, mind and soul working as one. These important aspects of our lives need to be taken care of. More importantly, they need to be balanced, because, when that happens, each category strengthens the others, and we become far greater than the sum of our parts.

For example, if your career and finances are in good order, the lack of stress in these areas may help you be more family-oriented. A good family life may inspire you to take better care of your health so you can be strong and healthy for your loved ones. Better health will allow you to have more energy and a positive attitude to focus on your career and finances and, of course, your family. In other words, a better mind will help create a better soul, a better soul will help create a better body and a better body will help create a better mind, and on it goes.

To truly maximize your potential, determine which aspects of your life are most important and learn to balance them. One way to do this is by reducing or cutting things out of your life that you don't need.

In the late 1800s, an Italian economist named Vilfredo Pareto published a paper while at the University of Lausanne. In his paper, he showed that 80% of the land in Italy was owned by only 20% of the population. Over the years, management consultants noticed that this 80/20 imbalance applies to many other aspects of life and business. This is referred to as the Pareto Principle or the 80/20 rule. For example, most of our closet space is often taken up by what we wear the least, and many companies make most of their money from a small percentage of their client base.

Likewise, many people spend the bulk of their time doing what they'd rather not be doing.

Imagine how much happier you'd be if you cut unnecessary or less enjoyable activities and spent more time on what you enjoy most. Of course you can't cut out everything you don't like. Just because you don't like doing chores at home doesn't mean you can neglect your duties. However, by learning what makes you truly happy, you can start maximizing the time you spend on those fulfilling things and minimize the rest.

At one point in my career, I worked for an organization that made presenting part of my job. I loved presenting. I didn't care if it was for sales or training, as long as I got to present, I knew I was going to have a good day.

However, I had many other responsibilities in that organization, such as filing numerous reports and attending numerous meetings. Presenting was actually a very small part of my job. Once I realized what I really loved to do, I found a job where it was my main focus. I wasn't able to cut reports and meetings out of my life entirely, but I found a way to minimize what I didn't like and maximize what I did.

In doing so, not only was I happier, I was also more successful. My employer loved my presentation style, and, since presenting made up most of my job, I excelled in that organization. Not to mention I was also able to sharpen my presentation skills even further.

The first step for you to amplify the aspects of your life that make you happy is to figure out what they are. What are your passions, goals and desires?

Most of the time we know what they are but just haven't taken the time to write them down. While we are unlikely to go grocery shopping without a grocery list, too many of us attempt to get through life without a life list. Why do we put more care in to our grocery-shopping strategies than our life strategies?

Figure out what your goals are for your body, mind and soul and write them down. What is that 20% of your life you would rather be doing 80% of the time? Going through this process will help you let go of or reduce the things you don't need and move more quickly towards your goals. It's not unlike what I said in chapter 3 about understanding your caloric goals and tracking them, what I said in chapter 6 about tracking your obligations, and what I said in chapter 11 about your savings goals.

It all comes from the same principle. It's all connected. We can't move towards something we like and cut something we don't unless we know what we like and don't like.

By constantly reviewing your goals, you'll not only get into the habit of working towards them but you'll also integrate them into your belief system. This is where the power really lies.

When I was younger, my parents were strict about my saying thank you when I received a gift. Eventually it became a habit. Without even thinking about it, I responded with thanks whenever someone gave me something. However, as important as good habits are, they should not be the end goal. It wasn't until I got a bit older that I learned the true magic of saying thank you. Good manners are now way beyond habit to me. They're part of my core belief system.

If you want to be good, make tracking and working towards your goals a habit. If you want to be great, make this process a part of your core beliefs. The best way to do this is by cutting things from the 80% of your life that aren't very important to you. Cut and reduce what you can, focus on what remains and you will find happiness.

In addition to tracking your goals, track your accomplishments. This way, when you're having a bad day or need some motivation, you can look at your lists and see what you've accomplished and what you still want to reach. Do this and you won't get stuck in a vicious circle of chasing things that don't benefit you.

I also like to track my good days. More importantly, I like to analyze them. I ask myself: What do I do on a good day that makes me happy? How do I act? And what is in my control that I can do on a bad day to make myself happy when I need to?

I've noticed that, when I'm in a good mood or feeling confident, I tend to speak very loudly (or so I've been told). I become very social and like to joke around. Once I realized this was my behavior when I was in a good mood, I started mimicking this behavior when I was in a bad mood.

I remember a terrible morning when my alarm clock didn't go off when it should have, or maybe it did and I ignored it; I dropped my coffee and spilled it all over my pants; and I battled traffic and barely made it to work on a day when I had a full schedule of presentations ahead of me. I was anxious, nervous and even a bit angry. I felt very small, very quiet and anti-social – all of the things that are the opposite of a happy me.

I could have gone down this path and let my negativity snowball, but instead I started employing some of my happy behaviors even though I wasn't feeling them.

The first thing I did was force myself to converse with some of my colleagues. I made small talk about my morning and even made some jokes about my coffee pants. I immediately started to feel better. I knew a happy me was a loud me, so I started calling out greetings to people as I walked through the halls in the friendliest voice I could muster.

By the time I got to my office, I was practically shouting, not like a crazy man but like a very friendly man who's only sort of crazy. However silly I may have seemed, my loud speaking, socializing and joking around put me in a good mood and prepared me for the day to come.

In chapter 7 I focused on the importance of developing a communication formula so you can sound good consistently. What I'm talking about here is similar – developing your very own "good day" formula. Speaking loudly, socializing and joking around works for me, but it may not work for you. As you start analyzing your goals and desires, analyze your behaviors, as well. Ask yourself how you act when you're in a good mood. Start employing that behavior more often, even if it's forced. In many cases, this will begin to change the way you feel.

As you analyze your behaviors, be sure to also look at your negative behaviors. Learn what they are and work to reduce them. For me, it's being quiet. A weak and sad me is a quiet me. The minute I feel that coming on, I know I must eliminate all things quiet or I'll start going down a long negative path.

By encouraging you to let go of things or cut things that don't bring you happiness and success, I'm referring not only to tasks or habits but also to emotions and behaviors. We've all had points in our life when something makes us incredibly angry. Anger is a poison that can affect us physically, mentally and spiritually.

One time I had this really tight muscle – right on my butt cheek, of all places. Sitting down on a chair was like plumping myself down on a sharp rock. As embarrassing as it was to tell a massage therapist I needed help with my butt cheek, the pain was worse. She had to massage the knot and make it soft so the pain would go away.

Some people need to get their emotional pain massaged. They may think holding on to their anger makes them strong by keeping them hard. They go through life becoming harder and harder emotionally. But I can say from first-hand experience that the hardness that's built up this way is actually what's *causing* their pain.

Sometimes the pain we experience is a literal pain in the butt and sometimes it's some jerk who's really bugging us. In either case, staying hard is not going to help. Let me encourage you to let go of those negative emotions. Focus your attention on yourself and your loved ones. You'll feel a great weight being lifted from you, not to mention greater comfort when you sit down.

You can actually *prevent* anger from building up, by understanding how many of the negative things that happen to you are usually not personal. When someone cuts you off on the road, you accuse them of all kinds of evil intent. But they probably didn't even realize they did it, or, if they did, they didn't know who they did it to. It wasn't personal.

Don't let anger over such things eat at you. In the vast majority of cases, it's not personal.

In the event that it *is* personal and someone *is* giving you a hard time, consider this: if the world weren't filled with so many unpleasant people, it wouldn't be so easy for you to make someone's day by complimenting them. The person who's bothering you makes you stand out when you show a positive attitude.

And don't carry the anger with you to someone who had nothing to do with it. Instead, be happy to be speaking with someone different. Tell them it's great to talk to them. The reaction you receive will help you get over the unpleasant interaction you just had. It may even make it easier for you to forgive the person who wronged you, helping you let go of that negative energy.

If you're angry about something that's not necessarily personal but related to the world in general – for example, social, economic or environmental injustices – then turn your anger into positive energy. Do something about the issue you're concerned about. Focus on the positive change you plan to make and get to work to make it happen.

Sometimes anger lingers when we constantly relive a particular memory or thought. How many times has this happened to you? Maybe you're stuck in traffic and, as you sit there alone with your thoughts, you start thinking about something from the previous week or a few months ago or even a few years ago. Maybe it's about a time someone upset you. Maybe it's about a friend of yours who weaseled his way out of splitting the dinner tab again. Maybe it's about a family member who broke another promise.

As you sit there stewing over this, your anger grows. It wasn't a major issue before you got in your car, but now your anger is building on itself. You start driving a bit more aggressively and honk at other cars. And they start honking at you.

When you finally make it to work, you act rudely to your colleagues. They respond by being rude right back to you, and it makes you feel even worse.

And it all started from something your brain brought to mind only because you were bored.

When I begin to focus on a memory that makes me angry or even frightens me, I immediately change my thought process and linger over good things instead. Focusing on a memory that makes me happy or an event that gives me confidence or strength makes me start to feel good again.

The bad news is we all have the incredibly destructive

ability to make ourselves angry over something from the past that doesn't currently have any real immediate impact on us. However, the good news is that this also works in reverse. We have the incredibly beautiful ability to make ourselves happy and confident, even if only briefly, by reflecting on positive thoughts or memories.

If you find yourself alone and your head becomes filled with thoughts, you won't always be able to eliminate the bad ones. But with a constant review of your goals, desires, positive behaviors and accomplishments, it's very possible for you to replace them with good thoughts and memories. Use that as your fuel for taking on the day and taking back your life.

Sometimes a bad memory is connected to a specific person. In severe situations, we need to cut people out of our lives, for our sanity or even our physical safety. That being said, some people are a bit too quick to pull this trigger. The minute someone remotely upsets them, they cut that person out of their life. Do this enough and you'll find yourself alone.

Where possible, cut out the anger and hate but don't cut out the person. Often all it takes is avoiding the situations that make you angry with that person. For example, if you hate going to a restaurant with a friend who never pays his portion of the bill, even if you bring it up to him, stop going to restaurants together. Find new activities you can enjoy together that don't trigger your frustration.

Unfortunately, many people do the opposite: they cut out the person but carry a burden of hate long after the person who caused it is out of their lives. Their hatred brings them nothing but pain. You may not be able to forgive someone or have them back in your life, but you can let go of the hate. The negative energy is a cancer in your life. It has no benefit for you.

This may be harder for some than others. I encourage you, if you can't let go of hate, to see a therapist. Unfortunately, in our society, even though therapy has become more common, people are often ashamed to seek this kind of help. But if it's acceptable to work with a personal trainer to improve your body, why not work with someone to improve your mind and soul?

What about when *we're* the ones being cut out of someone's life? This situation can be very difficult, especially when we don't know why. If we're given a reason why the relationship needs to change, we can try to explain why we did what we did. We can apologize for it, attempt to fix it and make sure we don't do it again. Or, at the very least, we can give a proper goodbye. When we don't know, it can drive us a bit crazy.

If you're in this situation and you've tried to find out what went wrong but aren't getting any answers, do yourself a favor. Accept that the relationship is over and move on. Constantly trying to contact them will drive you both insane and do nothing to resolve the matter. Sometimes people enter our lives for a reason or purpose, and when that reason or purpose is no longer there, they move on. Sometimes we need to cut them out of our lives. Sometimes they cut us out of theirs. Instead of being angry for being the one cut out, focus on the good times you had with that person and move on. Put your energy and love in to those who are still in your life.

There are also situations where we need to cut relationships before they even begin.

A friend of mine hates to drink and party but somehow

always dates women who love the club scene. He figures if he likes everything else about a woman, he can give the relationship a try and eventually she'll come around and adapt to his lifestyle. Sometimes he tries to tell the woman what to do. Sometimes the woman tries to make him more of a party animal. Either way, it always results in frustration, pain and a break-up.

I'm not saying you shouldn't date people who have different hobbies and interests. Just be careful of situations where the differences are so great you or the other person has to change, because that's a problem, one that will only grow with time.

Just as you shouldn't have to change to fit another person's interests and lifestyle, they shouldn't have to change to fit yours. There are plenty of people out there who are a good match for you.

The theme of this chapter is really all about analyzing yourself and asking yourself what your goals and desires are and, just as importantly, what you want to move away from. This kind of understanding will help you move towards what or who will make you happy and avoid what or who won't.

Let's say saving money is important to you, and you just started dating someone who loves to blow through their money. Ask yourself, "Am I okay with this?" If so, great. If not, just remember that trying to change the other person's personality and habits isn't the solution. Build a solid understanding of what your relationship deal-breakers are and look for them early to prevent heartaches later.

As you make your list of where you want to spend

your time and attention, don't forget to include taking some time for yourself. I'm not just talking about time to study or work out but about time to relax and do nothing and only focus on you. Whenever I'm on a plane, I'm reminded that focusing on ourselves isn't necessarily selfish. Before takeoff, they always announce that, in the event of an emergency, passengers should apply their own oxygen mask before helping others with theirs. We're not going to be any good to anyone if we pass out.

The same goes for life. To help our friends and family the best we can, we need to take time for ourselves every now and then, otherwise we'll burn out or negative emotion will set in. When creating an overall balance strategy, me time is part of what needs to be balanced with everything else.

So go ahead, have that glass of wine, schedule some time at the spa, play a round of golf – you've earned it because you're awesome!

14

Doing What Nike Says

*T*HROUGHOUT this book, we've looked at many tips and tricks for tackling life and becoming awesome at being awesome. We've covered calorie counting, career building, personal life improvement and how to stay positive, communicate effectively, manage money and much more. We've also covered how to tie it all together and reduce everything we don't need.

But after all of our reading and planning, after all of our lists are made, we now have to do what Nike says. We have to Just Do It.

I know what you're thinking: I can't believe this guy is quoting a corporate slogan! But it really does define what needs to happen next. Research and planning are absolutely essential, but nothing happens until you actually do something.

For example, in chapter 3 I mentioned the benefits of calorie counting. This strategy has done wonders for me. However, a lot of diet enthusiasts hate this method, and there's no end to the debates about which diet method is better. The truth is, any plan will work. You just need to do it. Anything worth doing will require time and effort. But mostly it will require actually starting the process and sticking to it. If you hate calorie counting, you can throw a rock out the window and hit another diet plan that can help. Please note: I do not endorse rock throwing out of any window in any way! What I'm trying to say is that, whatever diet plan you choose, make sure you actually start it and stick to it.

Nothing happens until we do something. This is true for all aspects of our lives.

By sixth grade, I had become known as a class clown. My parents graciously made sure to supply me with never-ending material. I happily shared my stories of Bon Jovi T-shirts and white skates to anyone who would listen – I guess I still do. I've even written a children's book version of the skate story (not yet published – *hint, hint* to anyone out there who may be interested).

As I got a bit older, I started hanging out with other class clowns. Since we were always goofing around, we often talked about how great it would be to do an act at a comedy club. This, of course would take some nerve. It's one thing to be the funny guy in a group of friends or a class and quite another to prepare a routine, get up on stage and make a bunch of strangers laugh.

Finding a club that will let you to try out your material is the easy part. Most comedy clubs have an open mic night where anyone can perform for five minutes. The hard part is actually doing it. For something like this, you can prepare all you want by researching comedy clubs and rehearsing your material over and over, but ultimately you need to actually go through with it. This is what separates those who achieve what they want from those who don't.

My fellow class clowns and I graduated from high school in 1995. None of my buddies ever went forward with doing a comedy show. I myself didn't get around to doing it until 2002. It took me seven years to work up my nerve. But once I got a taste, I realized how enjoyable it was. I've been back many times and even headlined my own show more than once.

From my first amateur comedy night and on, I noticed something very interesting. Whenever someone found out I did stand-up, they always got really excited and told me how much they respected the fact I did it. They asked me a ton of questions about the experience. But the one question no one has ever asked in the more than 10 years since I've been doing stand-up is whether I'm any good.

This has been such a beautiful lesson for me. There are some things we're afraid of doing because we fear not being any good. But at the end of the day, most people care very little about whether we're any good. For the most part, they're impressed by the fact we actually did it.

For a lot of people, the Just Do It concept is painful. I've had jobs where certain colleagues' main purpose in life was to slack off. They got to work with one goal, doing the least amount of work possible. It sounds like it could be fun, especially when you get paid the same amount as the people really sweating it. But here's the problem: I've never met a slacker employee who was happy. By making it their only goal to work as little as possible, they deprive themselves of purpose. As much as we think a life without responsibility would be amazing, ultimately it's not what any of us really wants.

Sadly, though, slacking off is how many people live their lives. They go through their days looking to do as little as possible, thinking a life of leisure will bring them happiness. This is not the case.

Have you ever been driving for a long time and then been unable to remember the last 15 minutes? You zoned out for a while because the drive itself took very little effort. It's so routine that everything becomes automatic.

This is how many people live. One year turns into the next, things get so routine that everything becomes automatic. Before they know it, a decade has gone by, and they have nothing to show for it. Don't let this happen to you.

What sometimes interferes with our ability to Just Do It is our amazing capacity to question something to death. An opportunity comes our way, and all we do is overthink it. As mentioned in chapter 5, we can't see the opportunity past the problem. We over-research by asking numerous "why" questions, such as, "Why should I bother doing this project?" Instead, we need to ask ourselves, "Why not?" Sometimes we need to get our head out of our butt, stop making excuses, stop looking for problems, stop questioning things and just get to work.

Another big problem that interferes with our ability to Just Do It is waiting for someone or something to come save us. Since we're waiting for a hero, we don't plan anything ourselves, let alone put it in to action.

Back in 1993, a movie came out called *Alive*, based

on the true story of a Uruguayan rugby team stranded in the Andes Mountains after their plane goes down. To survive, the team is forced to do some intense things.

At one point, one of the main characters, Nando, played by Ethan Hawke, announces to everyone that he's been listening to the radio and has good news: the rescue party that's been looking for them has just been cancelled. No one will be coming.

This of course upsets all of the other survivors.

"Why the hell is that good news?" one of them asks.

"Now we know it is up to us to get out of here," Nando says.

That line hit me like a ton of bricks. Since then, anytime I come to a point of darkness or uncertainty, I repeat to myself, "No one is coming to save me, and that's good news. It's up to me!"

Some may feel a statement like this must come from someone who's not a team player or doesn't have strong ties to their family or maybe doesn't have much faith. That couldn't be further from the truth. I love being a part of a team. I love my family and have a great relationship with them and my close friends. I also happen to be a man of faith.

The line "no one is coming to save me" is a way of saying I will not blame anyone for my failures nor will I rely on anyone else for my success. It doesn't mean I won't ask for help numerous times a day or won't pray for a miracle from time to time. It means – and this gives me great comfort – that getting myself to where I need to be is up to me.

When I was younger, I hated school for a slew of reasons. In addition to my problems with bullies, I was a terrible reader. My parents didn't understand English very well but tried to help me as best as they could to improve my grades. But having someone who doesn't understand English teaching you to read English is not such a great idea. As you can guess, those lessons were very painful for me and my parents. I was a terrible student, always sneaking away from my lessons and not wanting to participate.

Then one day my parents came up with a brilliant plan – to invite a family friend over to help me study. He was a bit older than I was and had a knack for teaching, plus he got good grades. His name was Johnny.

The minute my parents told me their plan, I thought, "Great! Now I don't have to worry or try at all because my buddy Johnny is gonna get me those good grades." I took my friend's generous help and turned it into something negative. All I wanted to do was play. Anytime someone said to me, "You need to study," I just replied, "Don't worry, Johnny will take care of it."

Eventually my mom hit me with some pretty good mom wisdom: "Why should Johnny put in an effort to help you when you're not putting in an effort to help yourself? People are here to help you – your friend Johnny, your teachers at school, your parents, your sisters – but ultimately it's up to you. We can't help you if you don't help yourself."

Even as a kid who was mad at his mom for making him study, I knew she was on to something. Although I wasn't about to admit it to her at the time, she was right, and that moment stayed with me.

Like my younger self waiting to be saved by a friend, a lot of adults look to others to "fix" them. Let's take a look at the multimillion-dollar industry of diet pills. I always take great pleasure in watching commercials about these pills, not because I believe in the products but because I find them so amusing. Some of the commercials say take this pill and you can eat whatever you want. They show models lapping up ice cream and scarfing down hamburgers and tell us they didn't have to even exercise to lose the extra pounds. But wait, there's more! Not only did their weight miraculously come off, but they also magically got abs. And all they did was take a pill.

Wouldn't that be nice? Sit back, relax, do absolutely nothing except take a magic pill and you'll be saved. Instead of waiting for this false savior, take a step back, do the research, put a plan in place and get to work. You can achieve the results you want, but it's up to you to do the work.

Another good example of false saviors is any get-rich-quick scheme. This is another industry responsible for some great commercials. Following a very similar formula, they promise both amazing and immediate results with virtually no work.

One commercial in particular got my attention. I was amazed by its bold claims. I decided to order the investment strategy product it was pushing, not because I thought it would make me rich but because I wanted to research and write about it. One of the commercial's claims was that one of its participants made a $20,000 profit their first week. When I got the package, it was so thick, I didn't know how anyone could read so much material in one week let alone implement any of its strategies.

Eventually, after I had waded through it all, I started

to test the system in every way possible. As I suspected, it was utter nonsense. The system was a complete waste of time and money (other than being good for a laugh). Yet this system is one of the more popular get-rich-quick schemes out there. Millions of dollars are made off people who want to get rich without working for it. If you're one of them, instead of wasting your time and money on these kits, why not put some real effort in to career improvement and financial planning? Doing so will bring you much closer to achieving the success you're looking for.

The girl in Robert Munsch's children's book *The Paper Bag Princess* ends up not only becoming her own hero but also saving the day and the prince, and all because she didn't wait to be saved – she knew it was up to her. That's what we need to be like. We need to be our own hero because no one else is coming. It's okay to be a hero to others, and it's okay to have a hero, but don't sit around waiting to be saved. You'll be much happier by taking control of your own life. Not only will you improve your chances of success, but you also won't be burdened with blaming others.

Often when we wait for a hero and are disappointed, we start to blame others for our failures or lack of happiness. Anytime I've ever come across someone who blames others in this way, I notice that their blame eventually turns into incredible anger and then hate, which does nothing for them.

Are you like this? Instead of wasting that energy on those negative feelings, put it towards achieving the success you want.

At one point in my career, I had a colleague who was working on a sale with a potential client but he admitted to not having done the work you need to do to ensure a sale. He eventually scheduled a meeting for me to present a demo to the client, figuring my presentation would impress them so much they'd look past his slacking off and award him the sale.

This, of course, didn't happen. And instead of taking ownership of the fact that he didn't spend enough time researching or speaking with the client to understand their needs, my friend was upset with me for not delivering a presentation that resulted in a win. On top of that, he was upset with his boss for not authorizing lower pricing. I should point out that his boss had been known to authorize lower pricing but only if a sales rep could explain the situation, which this rep was never able to do because...well, that would have taken too much effort.

The rep had a long list of complaints against a long list of people, except he missed the most important person – himself. He refused to discuss what he could have done better and how he would approach things differently the next time.

This way of thinking can prevent us from moving forward and learning from an experience in order to avoid repeating mistakes in the future. If we focus solely on how angry we are or how others are to blame, we can't possibly take the measures necessary to achieve success.

The workplace is a breeding ground for blame. I have heard every possible complaint there is:

"I hate my job."

"I hate my boss."

"These guys are so stupid!"

What always puzzles me is why the people who complain the most about their job never actually leave the company. If it's so terrible, why are they still there?

One of my friends went on a rant while we were having lunch at a restaurant. Becoming more and more drunk, he just kept complaining about his boss. This wasn't the first time I had seen him drink too much during business hours. Admittedly, his boss was tough on him, but that was no wonder. My friend refused to take any responsibility for his slacking off on the job and being a fairly lousy employee overall. He was frequently late to work, missed deadlines and on occasion got a little tipsy right in the office.

Perhaps his company's real flaw wasn't anything he thought they needed to change. Maybe it was that they let him keep his job.

This employee was stuck in a cycle of hate, doing nothing to better his company and doing nothing to better his own happiness. He also happened to complain about his weight gain, poor finances and ungrateful family – proof that an unproductive and negative attitude in one part of life will spill over into other parts.

Let's take a look at this blame game from another point of view by considering again the documentary *Super Size Me*. In the film, we hear from young ladies who are suing McDonald's because they blame the fast food chain for their weight gain.

This completely absurd way of thinking is a perfect example of what I'm talking about. Unless someone had a gun to their head and was forcing them to eat those Big Macs and drink those sugary drinks, how could they possibly blame someone else for their weight gain? Their blame game is getting in the way of their achieving what they actually want – losing weight. No lawsuit is going to help them with that – a lawyer is certainly not going to give them advice on weight loss. Instead of being upset and playing the part of the victim, they should get to work.

Another target of blame I often hear about is parents. I don't have any kids myself, but I have to say I feel sorry for parents. They seem to get blamed for all the problems of the world. We've all done it, myself included. People blame their parents for their lack of success, their unhappy relationships or the lack of anything good in their lives. Some people seem to think anything bad that's ever happened to them can somehow be traced back to something terrible their parents did to them when they were kids.

When I was younger, my dad was my dentist. He was actually the dentist for all the neighborhood kids. You may be thinking, "Wait a second, didn't you say you came from a poor family? Dentists usually do pretty well for themselves."

Let me clarify. When I say my dad was a dentist, I don't mean he was a real dentist with a lab coat and dental license. (Do dentists have licenses? Not sure.) What I mean is he was the guy who pulled our teeth out when they were loose. His dental tools? A string, a door and a chair. He'd sit you down on the chair, tie a string to your tooth and to the door and then slam the door shut, removing the loose tooth and possibly some that weren't loose at all. Our chances of growing up with a crooked smile were pretty much guaranteed.

I could let that bother me and go on and on about how my parents ruined my smile. Or I can be adult about it and go see a real dentist to fix my teeth if it bothers me that much. For now, I'm keeping my crooked teeth and strategically smiling in photos, all while not complaining.

Some people's parents really did drop the ball. There are extreme circumstances when parents *have* ruined their kids' lives. But whether you're a child of extreme circumstance or someone like me with the occasional parental complaint that's really more of a funny story, there comes a time when you need to stop blaming your parents and start working on what happens next. The next steps could be difficult and involve getting professional help, including things like therapy and medication. Whatever the case, research the next steps, make a plan, make a list and get to work.

When we believe others are at fault for our misery, we waste energy and time on hate and anger towards them. We may temporarily feel better, but this wasted energy brings us no closer to getting what we actually want. The truth is, it doesn't matter whose fault it is. Whether the fault is ours or someone else's, beating ourselves up or beating someone else up (literally or figuratively) will get us nowhere.

We need to focus on what the problem is and what is in our control to fix. That's why I hold only myself accountable for my failures. I know that ultimately I can control only myself. Of course many things outside myself are out of my control, but why on earth should I waste energy on something I can't do anything about?

When something doesn't go the way I planned, I analyze the situation, find out what went wrong and start to make a plan and a list – or a series of lists – about what I'm going to do differently next time. Then I get to work on making sure it doesn't happen again.

Two things to take from this are:

1. Blaming anyone, even yourself, will do you no good.

2. If it's not in your control to fix something, then it makes no sense to waste your energy on it. Focus on yourself and what you can control, and the other pieces will fall into place.

The concept of Just Do It in this chapter is to avoid the things that get in your way like waiting to be saved and blaming others for your failures. It's also important to examine envy. Like blame, envy leads us down a path of wasted time and energy, away from getting what we want. It's often part of the same or at least a very similar conversation. Whenever I hear someone blame others for their lack of success or happiness, I often sense some envy as well.

Envy has been around for a long time. I'm pretty sure it was born the first time one caveman brought home a bigger animal to eat than his neighbor did. In this day and age, envy seems more common than ever. With social media, we don't need to actually talk to or even interact with our friends and family to be envious. All we need to do is log on to our chosen social media platform, and we can be envious anytime we want, 24/7. Envy is just a click away.

Many times this makes us want to compete on social

media. We see something that makes us envious and we want to put up a picture showing how great our lives are, how happy we are. Sometimes I scroll through my social media feed and see someone has written something along the lines of, "Out with friends and having the best time!" I'm always so amused by that. You mean to tell me you're having such an amazing time you feel the need to interrupt your amazing time to post something online about it? It's almost as if they think that, if no one sees it, their good time doesn't matter.

This makes no sense to me. While this may not be the worst thing in the grand scheme of things, it does get in the way of people actually living their life. Why on earth would we let feelings caused by an outside source interfere with our having a good time?

I can't count the number of times I've seen people at a party stop their fun to pose for multiple pictures, so they can get the perfect party shot to post online – one where they look like they're having the time of their lives and, more importantly, look great having it. Here's an idea: Why not just focus on having a good time? Shouldn't the goal be to have an actual good time, not to make others *believe* you're having one?

I've noticed something else about negative competition and envy: we often feel these emotions in connection with the people closest to us. This is probably why social media can make us so crazy. We have a constant window into our friends and their "amazing" lives. Generally we're not envious of celebrities or people far removed from us. However, when a friend or a "frenemy" gets something we want, that can drive us crazy. We might think, "This person is like me, we're from the same circle, yet they've accomplished something I didn't. Why couldn't I have done that?"

Similarly, someone close to us may have lost a lot of weight or gotten a big job promotion and posted all about it on social media. Envy transforms this good news into something ugly that eats us up inside. These feelings wear us down because we can't discuss them with anyone. We realize our negative feelings are a result of immature envy and of course we could never admit that in a million years. Instead, we come up with other reasons why we hate this person and believe we're completely justified in feeling this way.

The result? We become a poor friend to this person who did nothing wrong and wear ourselves out in the process.

I mentioned earlier how we need to be our own hero. In this case, not only are we not the hero, we're also the villain.

But that's okay. All of us have played the part of the villain at one point in our lives. It comes with being human, and there's a way to deal with these feelings so we can be the hero again. It's a technique I've used since childhood.

I have a million flaws. Ask my wife and she'll up that to a billion, but even she will tell you I seem to be immune to envy. The secret to my immunity is something I admitted to in chapter 1 – how I hound anyone I sense can give me good advice. If someone accomplishes something I want to accomplish, I ask them how they did it. When I see someone with something I want, I don't see a problem. I see an opportunity – an opportunity to ask someone for help.

If you find yourself feeling envious, turn that envy into motivation. Whenever possible, get over your own ego and ask for help and guidance. Use what others have learned to help you achieve what you want. Most people will gladly share their secrets of success. Often all it will cost you is a compliment.

If you feel you don't need advice, there's nothing to be envious of, so you need to let it go. Or if the friend doesn't want to give you guidance, don't worry about it. There's no shortage today of information on any topic you want to learn about. Use the motivation of your friend's success and find the information yourself online (or in this awesome book!).

Envy also seems to be at its most powerful and hurtful when someone in our circle begins to succeed in areas we may be best known for.

Maybe you like hosting dinner parties and you're known among your friends as being a Martha Stewart type. Then all of a sudden, a good friend hosts an amazing dinner party that everyone loves and it's killing you.

Perhaps you're the athlete of your group, and then a friend who was never particularly athletic trains for and wins a sporting event. Everyone is so happy for them – except you, because it's killing you inside.

Or the slacker in your group suddenly becomes a vice president of a major company, making you feel small.

These feelings eventually turn into hate and are of no benefit to you or your friends.

The first thing to do is remind yourself that your envy isn't an exterior problem; it's an interior problem. In each of these cases, it's not your friend's fault that you feel this way. It's your fault because of your perception of the situation. If you let go of the anger and focus instead on being happy for your friend, you'll reduce your feelings of envy.

The second thing is to remind yourself it's not possible for anyone else's accomplishments to diminish your own. Nothing anyone else has done can possibly take away all of the awesomeness of what you've done.

Unfortunately, these two things are easier said than done.

I had a friend in sales who earned a good living, making about $100K a year. His wife worked in a non-sales office job, making about $60K a year. Working in this role, she became very familiar with her company's products, clients and processes. She had a great personality and decided to make the leap into sales. In her first year, she made $150K. As a couple, their combined income went up by $90K. That's unheard of.

But instead of seeing the benefit of his wife being very happy in a career she was clearly meant for, instead of appreciating the obvious benefit of having all this additional income, all my friend could focus on was how supposedly terrible it was to be out-earned by his wife.

This is a clear example of negative emotion getting in the way of reason. At first I was going to take my usual approach in these situations and encourage him to ask his wife for advice on how she did so well in her first year. But considering how upset he was, I had a feeling my advice not only would go unheard but also might get me punched in the face.

Sometimes when the source of our envy involves someone close to us, we struggle to overcome our ego and ask them for help, but when it's someone as close to us as a spouse, we can directly benefit from their success. In my friend's case, his wife's success and salary directly benefited him even if he failed to see it that way. If it was someone further removed from him, like a friend, it may not have hurt his ego as much, but his friend wouldn't have shared the wealth the way his wife would.

The way to get over envy is to see the opportunity beyond the perceived problem. In my friend's case, his wife's flourishing career was amazing news for his family. He would have been so much better off if he had let go of his envy altogether or had focused on achieving a more successful sales year himself.

Some people become envious over things that are beyond their control. They may think something like, "It's not fair. This person has rich parents and was born into such an easy life. Why can't my life be that easy?" Or, "That person has parents who help them out so much. Who's here to help me?" It's important here to remember this: We're always going to have people in our lives who have advantages we don't have, but there are also lots of people in our lives with disadvantages we don't have.

As a kid I heard a story from the New Testament about the owner of a vineyard who hired workers early in the morning to work that day for him for a denarius, a day's wage at the time.

Mid-morning, he hired some more workers and told them he would pay them whatever was right. Then he did the same thing at noon, three and five.

At the end of the day, he paid everyone the same: one denarius.

The people who worked the longest were upset when they found out they got paid the same amount as the group who worked the least. However, that all-day work crew had been happy with their pay until they learned what other people were earning.

If you're happy with your life, don't let the fact that someone has it better suddenly take that happiness away. Why let an outside factor determine how you feel about something you were previously satisfied with? Realize that you have it so much better than many others. Focus on seeing the good that's already in front of you, and you'll always have peace and happiness. And if something really is missing or not right with your life, find happiness in the fact that you have all of the abilities you need to change it.

Although I give awesome advice (see the rest of this book!), it doesn't always work equally well for everyone. If you've tried everything to get over your envy and nothing works, try to reduce the amount of time you spend with the person who brings it out in you. Even though the problem stems from you and not them, you're not doing yourself or them any favors by sticking around.

The same goes for those who may be envious of *you*. Don't take pleasure in making others envious. Try to avoid topics that you know will upset them. If, for example, they resent your career accomplishments, don't discuss your career with them. If you find it hard to not talk about certain things, and it really puts a strain on your relationship, consider reducing your time with them. As discussed in chapter 13, you need to focus on what's beneficial to you and cut out what isn't.

Like blame and envy, jealousy is also toxic, especially when it comes to romantic relationships. Many people find it difficult to deal with their partner getting attention from – or even interacting with – those they feel threatened by.

If this is true of you, first, ask yourself whether you trust the person you're with. If you do, there's no real reason to be jealous. Even if someone is blatantly interested in pursuing your partner, trusting your partner will keep you from letting outside forces affect how you feel.

Second, ask yourself whether the person you're with is intentionally doing something to get attention from someone else. That is, do they intentionally flirt all the time? If not, then the attention they're getting isn't their fault and shouldn't upset you. However, if they are a notorious flirt, discuss it at a time when you're both calm. Let them know how you feel without bringing insults into the conversation or raising your voice. Help them see the situation from your point of view.

And if you don't trust this person, and they don't respect your wishes, you have some thinking to do.

A relationship can't exist without trust and respect. You owe it to yourself to get that trust and respect, whether it be from the person you're with now or someone else. If you're the person doing the flirting, and it's really bothering your partner, do yourself and your partner a favor and stop. If you really need to flirt, maybe the relationship isn't for you.

Admittedly, after all is said and done, we can do our best to implement all the good life strategies we can think of, but dark days will still come. No matter what we do, no matter how happy and fulfilled we are, there will come a day that makes us question everything.

I hope it doesn't last long for you when it comes, but make no mistake, it's coming. Someone you love will die, something horrible you never thought possible will happen, and you will have a great need to be rescued. You will wait for a hero to save you, but that hero may never come.

I don't say this to scare or upset you. I say it to make you understand your true potential. You don't need to be rescued by someone else. *You* will be doing the rescuing, because you are awesome!

When my mom was dying, I was depressed, over-weight, financially strapped and on the verge of getting fired. I remember fantasizing about how great it would be to come across a magic genie. I would ask the genie to cure my mother and get me the body I wanted, along with a better career and more money. Other than the wish about my mom, I think most people would make very similar wishes if given the chance. This probably explains how industries related to these goals make so much money. However, when things are at their worst, there is no magic genie, pill or kit that can save you.

But, like Ethan Hawke's character in *Alive*, I've got some good news. You are going to save yourself. You don't need a genie, a magic pill or some get-rich-quick scheme. You can achieve the body, career and finances you want, but it's up to you. It will take time, and it will take effort. Use the techniques in this book: do the research, make a plan, make a list, balance what you need and cut out everything else.

And remember what Nike says – Just Do It!

15

Changing Yourself and the World

*T*HIS book was designed to help bring out your inner awesome by helping you find happiness, success, good health and balance with your body, mind and soul.

So how do we do that for the world? How do we bring out its inner awesome? How do we save it, how do we change it? Although the work is hard, the answer is actually very simple. The formula for a better world was written many years ago and it's something I first came across when I was a little kid. It's one of the most poetic, most profound and most important pieces of advice ever written: "Do unto others as you would have them do unto you."

I love this quote for two main reasons.

First, although it's from the Bible, it's not specific to any religion. It describes a way of life that's applicable to anyone regardless of their belief system.

Second, this one, short sentence describes the pathway to a better world. Think about it. If we all followed this way of thinking, if we all treated others the way we wanted to be treated, there would be no wars, no crime, no fighting. So many things in our world would improve.

We can look at this critically and think, "Why should I follow this way of life when, clearly, in a world filled with so much evil, no one else thinks like this?"

I encourage you to think differently. Don't let others stand in the way of your trying to make the world a better place.

If you can change just one person to think like this, even if that one person is only you, the world is one person better than it was before. Change one person, change the world. You have that power because you are awesome!

Resources for Weight Loss and Exercise

*A*N updated list of these sites and more can be found at www.AwesomeAtBeingAwesome.com.

MyFitnessPal

www.myfitnesspal.com

This one is by far my favorite. Easy to use, free and packed with information, MyFitnessPal is a mobile calorie and weight-tracking program. It can be accessed via computer or mobile app and is completely free. It features a large database, including brand name and restaurant foods, allowing you to easily keep track of regularly eaten food. Recipes and community groups are all part of this app and site as well.

Lose It!

www.loseit.com

Lose It! is a free mobile calorie-tracking program. It allows scanning of barcodes, tracking of your weight and joining groups with friends and even lets you partake in public challenges. There's a premium version for $39.99 a year that grants access to more features such as sleep tracking, exercise tracking, body measuring and macronutrients.

FitDay

http://www.fitday.com

FitDay is a free mobile weight and calorie-tracking program. Custom food can be inputted and custom goals can be created, and it has a really large food database. There are multiple premium versions that can be paid for access to features such as no ads, instant food additions and a live message board.

Calorie Counter by FatSecret

www.fatsecret.com

Calorie Counter by FatSecret is another free mobile app for tracking your weight and calories. It features a barcode scanner and manual barcode functionality. Some other features include recipes, food journals, an exercise diary, a food diary and information on popular restaurants and brands.

MyPlate Calorie Tracker by LIVESTRONG

www.livestrong.com/myplate

This app recently converted its premium version and its features into a free version. It features an extremely large food database to help with calorie and weight tracking. Personalized goals, water tracking and community connectivity are all also part of this app.

MyNetDiary
www.mynetdiary.com

This is another health and fitness app for tracking calories and weight. It features an offline mode, barcode scanning, macronutrient information and recipes. The pro version, which costs $3.99, includes more features like Fitbit integration and diabetes tracking information.

Calorie Counter by SparkPeople
www.sparkpeople.com/calorie-counter.asp

Another great free calorie and weight tracker in mobile form is Calorie Counter by SparkPeople. This app features a large food database, recipe integration, a barcode scanner and nutrient information.

Fooducate
www.fooducate.com

Fooducate is a free calorie and weight tracker. It has a food rating system, community recipe sharing, a barcode scanner and manual barcode capability.

Calorie Counter by Everyday Health
www.everydayhealth.com/calorie-counter

This free mobile app enables you to tailor and customize calories and meals. Calorie tracking, a large food database, recipes and customization, barcode scanning and regular reminders are just some of this app's features. One major aspect as well is offline access.

About the Author

*H*AVING to wear his older sisters' clothes to school because his parents felt that saving a few bucks was worth his utter humiliation, Danny Pehar learned to get through tough times by putting a comical spin on things.

Danny began his corporate life by taking an entry-level job so entry level he was told he needed to be promoted just to reach the bottom. Working his way up from underneath the bottom, he has sold and worked on multimillion-dollar projects as an entry-level employee, a manager, a director and an entrepreneur.

In addition to his business success, he is also a mixed martial arts enthusiast, a children's book author and a stand-up comedian with fans in Canada, Australia, Europe and the United States.

Whether he has succeeded as a champion or taken a brutal beating, Danny has a story to tell that will make you laugh, make you think and make you awesome!

www.AwesomeAtBeingAwesome.com

NOTES

NOTES